MW00897856

QUEENS
VICTORIA CROSSMAN

For Dave, Poppy and Evelyn

Published in the UK by Scholastic Children's Books, 2020
Euston House, 24 Eversholt Street, London, NW1 1DB

A division of Scholastic Limited
London – New York – Toronto – Sydney - Auckland
Mexico City – New Delhi – Hong Kong

SCHOLASTIC and associated logos are trademarks and/or
registered trademarks of Scholastic Inc.

Text and illustrations © Victoria Crossman, 2020

ISBN 978 0702 30190 2

A CIP catalogue record for this book is available from the British Library.

All rights reserved.

This book is sold subject to the condition that it shall not, by way of trade or
otherwise, be lent, hired out or otherwise circulated in any form of binding
or cover other than that in which it is published. No part of this publication
may be reproduced, stored in a retrieval system, or transmitted in any form
or by any other means (electronic, mechanical, photocopying, recording
or otherwise) without prior written permission of Scholastic Limited.

Any website addresses listed in the book are correct at the time of going
to print. However, please be aware that online content is subject to change
and websites can contain or offer content that is unsuitable for children.
We advise all children be supervised when using the internet.

Printed in China

1 3 5 7 9 10 8 6 4 2

www.scholastic.co.uk

QUEENS

VICTORIA CROSSMAN

■ SCHOLASTIC

CONTENTS

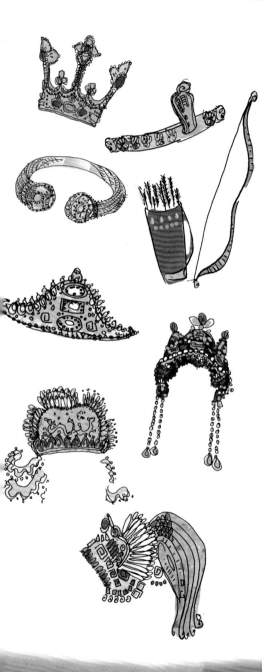

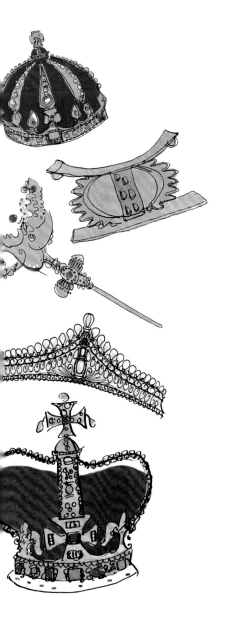

WELCOME

Get ready to dive in to the wondrous world of *Queens* – a **joyous roll call of women** who ruled kingdoms across the centuries and continents. From the **famous to the obscure**, these are stories of strength, resilience and sometimes cruelty, in societies where women were expected to be the fairer sex and to take their lead from men – but instead **rebelled to take power**.

Celebrate **Marie Antoinette**'s love of the lavish and extravagant, relish in **Tsarina Alexandra**'s stubborn refusal to toe the line and be wowed by Syrian warrior queen **Septimia Zenobia**'s fearless derring-do.

Equals to their male counterparts – about whom so much is already known and continues to be written – there is nothing meek or apologetic about these women.

Now is the time to hear their stories.

Now is the time for the queens.

Note to the Reader

Before you get started, please take a moment to read about the different types of queenly role. You can use the glossary (pages 144–47) to learn further detail about other words or terms used in the book.

Consort: the companion of a reigning monarch
Dowager: the widow of a late monarch
Regent: the person appointed to be head of state because the monarch is too young or unable to rule for another reason
Regnant: the ruling person.

QUEENS OF ANTIQUITY

Queen Neithhotep is believed to have been one of ancient Egypt's **first queens** in the Early Dynastic Period (*c.* 3150 BC).

Her alleged marriage to King Narmer united the two lands of Lower Egypt and Upper Egypt. The foundations of early civilization began with their union and it brought peace, order and trade.

Queen Hatshepsut was one of the most successful pharaohs in ancient Egypt. She became queen when she married her half-brother at the age of twelve. When her brother died in 1473 BC, she became regent to her stepson, and had the **power of a pharaoh**.

She can be seen in statues wearing a striped headcloth (*nemes*) and false beard, both of which are reserved only for the king.

Nefertiti ruled alongside her husband Akhenaten from 1353–1336 BC and it is thought she may have continued to rule after his death. She was queen at a time of **enormous change** in ancient Egypt.

Together they moved from worshipping the god Amon to the sun god Aten and changed the capital city of Egypt. She was known as her husband's '**great royal wife**' and together they had six daughters!

Teuta of Illyria lived in the third century BC, when the Romans controlled trade in the Mediterranean. She was married to King Agron of the Ardiaean kingdom and became queen regent for their son when Agron died suddenly in 231 BC.

Teuta was left in charge of a fleet of ships in the Adriatic Sea. This fleet was feared due to **pirating** and the many trade ships passing through were seen as easy pickings.

Traders were not happy with their ships being robbed and complained to the Roman politicians, who tried to make peace with Teuta. She chose to ignore this and allegedly killed one of the Romans. Outraged, they declared war and sent a fleet of over 200 ships and many soldiers to conquer Illyria. Unable to fight the might of the Roman army, Queen Teuta **surrendered**.

MAJESTIC MYTHS

**Myths are timeless tales that are widely
believed but not always true.**

According to folklore, **Queen Nur Jahan** of India saved an entire village that was being tormented by a large man-eating tiger. Being an **expert hunter**, she sat on an elephant, aimed her gun at the tiger … and shot it!

Legend has it that the courageous Syrian queen **Mavia** revolted against the Romans, leading her troops in **lightning attacks** that instilled fear into the bravest of soldiers. Realizing they could not defeat Mavia, the Romans finally called a truce.

The Roman historian, Dio Cassius, told a story of **Boudicca**, queen of the Iceni tribe in eastern Britain. Boudicca called to the ancient **goddess of victory**, Andraste, for help against the Romans in battle. She then released a hare from her cloak. The idea was that whichever side the hare ran towards would win the battle. The hare chose Boudicca and the Britons. The queen thanked Andraste … but lost the battle!

Empress Himiko, a ruler in third-century Japan, was believed to have practised magic as a **shaman queen**, going into trances to talk with the gods. She ruled jointly with her brother, but Himiko herself was rarely seen in public, safely housed with a thousand servants in the royal palace.

In the Icelandic sagas, **Queen Gunnhild** and her husband, King Eric Bloodaxe, were seen as **arch enemies** of the hero Egil Skallagrímsson. At a feast hosted by Gunnhild and Eric, Egil insulted them by saying their beer could not quench his thirst. They were so angry that they **poisoned his drink**. But he found out.

This set the scene for a **long-running feud**. Egil cast a curse and put a horse's head on a stick facing the sea. He then screamed the names of Gunnhild and Eric, asking the guardian spirits to drive them out of Norway. Their fate was now in the hands of the gods. It wasn't long before **disaster struck** ... and King Eric was dead.

THE QUEEN OF SHEBA

Mysterious visiting queen

Lived: tenth century BC

The Queen of Sheba is mentioned in both the Bible and the Qu'ran, and two countries – Ethiopia in northern Africa and Yemen in western Asia – claim to be her country of birth.

In Ethiopia, the Queen of Sheba, or Queen Makeda as she is also known, is a national legend. It is said that she once went to see King Solomon of Israel, who was known to be extremely wise. She arrived in a magnificent camel caravan with an abundance of jewels, gold and spices, and set Solomon some riddles to prove his wisdom. She stayed for six months, became pregnant with Solomon's son, Menelik, and then returned to Ethiopia.

When he was older, Menelik went to see his father. King Solomon was full of joy. When he returned to Ethiopia, Menelik took with him the Ark of the Covenant. The Ark was a golden chest containing two stone tablets with the Ten Commandments inscribed on them. Menelik became king – making the Queen of Sheba the nation's mother.

In Yemen, the Queen of Sheba is called Bilqis. In the Yemeni legend, King Solomon was told by a bird that there was a land ruled by a beautiful woman who worshipped the sun and moon. But he was warned that she was in fact a dangerous spirit, with hairy legs and cloven hooves!

An intrigued King Solomon sent an invitation for Bilqis to come and visit him. His palace floors were polished, so they shimmered like glass, and when Bilqis arrived, she thought it was a pool of water. So, she pulled up her skirt – revealing her hooves!

But nobody really knows the true story – to this day the Queen of Sheba remains a mystery.

SHE SET SOLOMON SOME RIDDLES...

REGAL BEAUTY

The beauty regimes of some queens were really quite out of this world! From using plant dyes to wearing towering wigs, noble women throughout history went to great lengths to maintain a superior look.

After surviving smallpox, **Queen Elizabeth I** was left with a scarred face. She would put white make-up on to cover the scars. This was called the '**mask of youth**'. Vinegar and lead were mixed together, which we now know would have caused damage to Elizabeth's health as the mixture gave off poisonous toxins. Her beauty regime took hours. Her lips were tinted red with plant dye, her eyes lined with kohl (a black powder), and her hair loss disguised by a red wig.

Marie Antoinette was famous for her towering bouffant hairdos known as '*monté au ciel*' ('ascended to heaven'). The wigs were made using scaffolding that was built around with hairpieces, then decorated with jewels, feathers, flowers and beads. The queen even used her **elaborate hairpiece** to celebrate the event of American independence from the British, with a replica of the French ship that had aided the American victory built into her wig!

Boudicca's English tribe, the Iceni, applied **blue warpaint** to their faces and bodies when preparing for battle. To make the paint, the leaves of the yellow-flowered woad plant were chopped up and made into a blue paste.

Egyptian queen **Cleopatra** would apply black kohl around her eyes with instruments made from ivory and wood. The Egyptians believed that it had magical **healing powers** against eye infections caused by the sand and flies. It also helped shield the eyes from the harsh glare of the sun.

In Chinese history, the precious jade stone symbolized beauty, nobility and wealth. **Empress Dowager Cixi** was rumoured to have had a small jade roller with a gold handle made to massage her face with, in the hope of maintaining her **youthful looks**.

CLEOPATRA
Flamboyant killer queen
Born c. 965 BC; died c. 931 BC

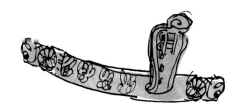

Cleopatra likened herself to the Egyptian goddess Isis, the nation's mother figure and protector. But she was involved in bloody rivalries. To some Cleopatra was an enlightened ruler and scholar; to others she was a seductress and killer queen.

Cleopatra is thought to have married her brother, Ptolemy VIII. Not long after their father's death, they became embroiled in a civil war. Cleopatra fled Egypt and formed her own army. Realizing that she needed the support of Rome to win back her throne, she devised a plan to meet the powerful Roman general, Julius Caesar.

She smuggled herself into Caesar's personal quarters inside a rolled-up carpet. But the powerful general was instantly smitten instead of surprised. They soon became partners, and under their joint rule Egypt thrived. Unfortunately, increasing tensions between Egypt and Rome ended with Caesar's assassination in 44 BC.

As Rome fell into civil war, Cleopatra was summoned to Tarsus in modern Turkey to meet the Roman general, Mark Antony. She arrived on a golden barge with purple sails, dressed as the goddess Aphrodite. She enchanted Antony, and together they ruled a prosperous Egypt.

But this wasn't to last. In 32 BC, the soon-to-be Roman emperor, Octavian, declared war and defeated Antony and Cleopatra. Antony and Cleopatra fled to Egypt. Here Antony heard the fake news that Cleopatra had died. Heartbroken, he took his own life.

Faced with capture, Cleopatra had a poisonous asp smuggled to her in a basket of figs. With one lethal bite, Cleopatra died. The last chapter of the pharaohs in ancient Egypt had ended.

Cleopatra and Mark Antony were buried together – archaeologists are still trying to find the burial chamber of the most famous lovers in history.

MAGNIFICENT MONEY

Throughout history, money has played an important part in spreading the fame of kings and queens. By having their portraits displayed on coins, monarchs ensured that they were always in the eye of the public.

A 1762 silver Russian ruble coin depicting **Catherine the Great**.

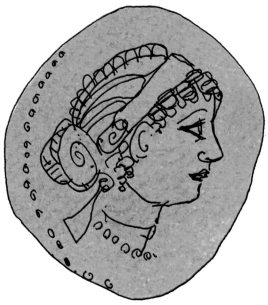

A bronze coin minted in Alexandria, Egypt (51–30 BC), showing **Cleopatra**.

The Riksdaler Coin, *c.* 1640, showing **Queen Christina Alexandra of Sweden**.

Queen **Nanny** of Jamaica was recognized as a national hero in 1976. Her portrait is featured on the $500 Jamaican banknote, which is fondly referred to as a 'Nanny'!

A gold coin minted in Alexandria, representing the Egyptian queen **Arsinoë II** (*c.* 316 BC–270 BC). It is thought to be the first coin featuring the portrait of a queen.

A coin showing **Queen Mary I**. She was the first queen regnant of England who ruled in her own right.

A gold coin struck at the Tower of London, featuring **Queen Elizabeth I**.

BOUDICCA
Britain's Celtic warrior queen
Born *c.* AD 30; died *c.* AD 61

Boudicca, the legendary Celtic queen, was married to Prasutagus, the ruler of the Iceni tribe in eastern Britain. When the Romans conquered Britain in AD 43, they allowed Prasutagus to continue his rule. Under Roman law, his lands would be passed to the Empire upon his death. Keen to outwit them, Prasutagus left half his land in his will to the Romans, and half to his two daughters.

After Prasutagus died, the Roman governor ignored his wishes and took everything, as well as stealing from the Icenis. Boudicca protested and was flogged.

Outraged, Boudicca led a rebellion against the Romans. In AD 61, her army attacked the Roman capital Camulodunum (modern-day Colchester), torching and destroying the town. The rebels continued on to Londinium (London) and Verulamium (St Albans).

The Roman general, Gaius Suetonius Paulinus, had gathered an army of 10,000 men to take on the rebels, and they finally clashed at the Battle of Watling Street. Boudicca urged her troops either to conquer or to die with glory. Dressed for battle, with blue-painted faces, they charged.

But against the might of the Imperial Roman army, the rebels didn't stand a chance. Suetonius had arrived early and chosen a battle location in a narrow valley, which protected his army from attack. The poorly equipped rebel army were cornered and slaughtered in their thousands.

Nobody knows what became of Boudicca. Some say she poisoned herself, others that she fell ill in battle and died.

NOBODY KNOWS WHAT BECAME OF BOUDICCA...

CROWNS FIT FOR A QUEEN

Crowns have always represented the power and glory of rulers around the world. They symbolize the royalty of the wearer and are often made from precious materials.

One of the oldest crowns in history is said to be the **Crown of Princess Blanche**, also known as the Bohemian Crown. Dating to around 1370, it most likely belonged to **Queen Anne of Bohemia**, wife of Richard II of England.

The **Imperial Crown of Russia** was worn by **Catherine the Great** on her coronation. It can now be seen in the Kremlin Armoury museum in Moscow, but was nearly sold off when the Romanovs were assassinated in 1918. When the crown was retrieved, it was only partially intact. The stones that had been removed and sold have since been replaced.

In 2017, **Queen Christina Alexandra of Sweden**'s crown was stolen from a cathedral. The thieves escaped by speedboat on the nearby lake. The crown was later discovered in a rubbish bin near Stockholm!

In 1661, Charles II of England had a crown made based on the eleventh-century Anglo-Saxon crown of Edward the Confessor. Called '**St Edward's Crown**', it is used in the coronation of all kings and **queens of England**. It is housed in the Tower of London along with the other Crown Jewels of the British monarchy.

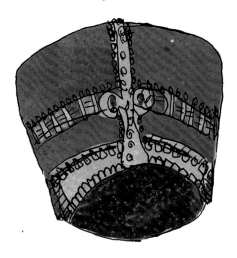

"I was a queen and you took away my crown." – attributed to **Marie Antoinette**.

The tall, flat-topped blue war crown of the ancient Egyptian queen, **Nefertiti**.

EMPRESS JINGŪ

Brave Japanese warrior

Born c. AD 170; died c. AD 269

Empress Jingū was a fabled queen who is said to have lived in third-century Japan.

Legend has it that she was the wife of Emperor Chūai, and after his death became empress regent for her son, Ōjin.

Jingū was said to be a shaman priestess who would go into trance-like states and communicate with the gods. She reigned during a period of unrest in Japan. When her husband died, she had declared war on Silla, a kingdom in ancient Korea. According to legend, she could control the tides by means of some magical jewels, which she used to defeat the Sillan army that was attacking her warships.

Stories are told that Jingū was pregnant by her husband before she set off for war. When she returned, the baby was born, after Jingū had been pregnant for three years! Some say that the child, Ōjin, was the Shinto god of war, Hachiman, and so was able to wait to be born when the war was over.

Many centuries later, in 1881, Jingū was the first woman to be featured on a Japanese bank note. But historians continue to question the existence of Empress Jingū, and in 1947 her name was removed from the official list of Japanese rulers.

A SHAMAN PRIESTESS...

ROYAL REBELS

Military might can be wielded by queens, not just by kings! Here are some examples of how powerful women have led the way in warfare.

Queen Isabella of Castile was rumoured to have loved the story of Joan of Arc. As a **wartime queen** in the 1400s, Isabella enjoyed planning military campaigns with her husband King Ferdinand. The cannons she used to blast castle walls were said to have changed the way that wars were fought.

Rani Lakshmibai fought an impressive campaign against the British in the Indian Mutiny of 1857. With her son tied to her back, a sword in each hand and the horse's reins between her teeth, she held onto the Jhansi Fort for weeks. Nearly a century later, the Indian National Army honoured her by forming the **Rani of Jhansi Regiment**, an all-female fighting unit.

On the death of her brother in 1576, **Queen Amina** of Zazzau (modern-day Nigeria) took the throne as the first queen of her people. A **fierce warrior**, respected throughout her country, she expanded the Hausa people's land through her many military campaigns, controlling an army of 20,000 men.

Rani Velu Nachiyar was the first Indian queen to fight against British colonialism in 1780. She was trained in martial arts, horse riding and archery. When her husband was killed by British soldiers she went with her daughter to find help. By building an army that included **female soldiers**, Rani Velu Nachiyar waged war against the British and regained her kingdom.

The rebellious Vietnamese **Trung sisters** were warrior women who fought for independence against the Chinese Han dynasty in AD 40. When one of their husbands was killed, they put together an army that included women and rode into battle **mounted on elephants**. The defeated Chinese fled. The sisters ruled an independent state for three years until they were finally defeated. Unable to face their fate, they took their own lives by jumping into the river. In Vietnam, their bravery is still celebrated today.

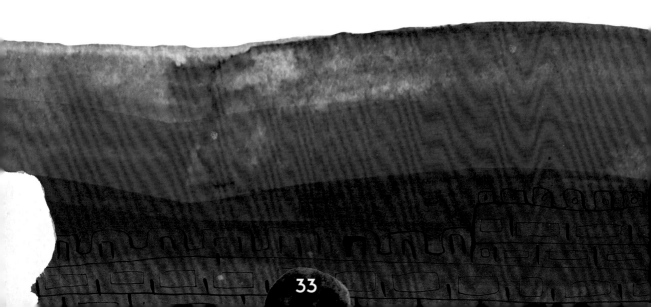

SEPTIMIA ZENOBIA
Rebel queen of Syria
Born c. AD 240; died c. AD 274

Septimia Zenobia was enchanting, fearless and rebellious. In AD 267, she declared herself queen regent for her young son, when her husband – Odaenathus, the ruler of Palmyra, Syria – was murdered.

Palmyra was on the Silk Road, at the crossroads between the Mediterranean lands dominated by Rome and the Persian Empire. The Silk Road was a route for traders, and this meant that Palmyra was a wealthy city, with magnificent buildings and impressive temples. During Zenobia's time, Palmyra was a client state – this meant it depended on and was controlled by Rome. Zenobia was keen to change this.

In AD 270, with Rome in a state of disorder, the defiant Zenobia seized her opportunity. She took the Eastern territories from Roman control and went on to take Egypt, too. This provided Palmyra with Egypt's wealth as well as control of the grain that was supplied from Egypt to Rome. This infuriated Rome as the grain made flour for bread, a staple of the Roman diet.

It seemed there was no stopping Zenobia, but the turning point came when Rome gained a new leader, Aurelian. He pushed Zenobia and her troops back to Palmyra, where she was captured.

Zenobia's death remains a mystery. Some say she took her own life. Others suggest her life was spared and she was given a villa near Rome. But the most common thought seems to be that Septimia Zenobia was brought to Rome in gold chains and banished to a palace where she quietly lived out the rest of her days.

The name Zenobia is nowadays used to describe an unstoppable, determined woman.

ENCHANTING, FEARLESS REBEL...

POWERFUL POLITICIANS

 William of Orange and **Mary II** of England signed a Bill of Rights in 1689, which gave more power to the English parliament. No longer would a king and queen of England have **absolute power**. This was the first step in creating the political system in Britain today.

 Queen Nur Jahan was one of the most powerful women in seventeenth-century India. She ruled – from behind a screen – over large areas of the Mughal Empire while her husband was ill. Nur Jahan was known to **help the poor** and support women's rights.

 A clever politician, **Queen Nzinga of Ndongo and Matamba** rebelled against Portuguese conquerors in the seventeenth century. She did this by building alliances and training runaway slaves to **fight with her**. Nzinga stopped the Portuguese from exploiting her people for the slave trade. Ndongo and Matamba – known today as Angola – went on to become an important trading hub.

 In 1588, **Queen Elizabeth I** addressed her troops before they fought against the Spanish Armada. Dressed in a white gown with a silver breast plate, she rode through the camp and said:

> *"I know I have the body of a weak and feeble woman, but I have the heart and stomach of a king [...]."*

When Elizabeth's navy defeated the Spanish, the 'Golden Age' of British history began.

As Russia's longest-reigning female leader until her death in 1796, **Catherine the Great** westernized the country and expanded the Russian Empire. **A gifted politician**, she wrote to famous writers of the time to improve Russia's image with the West. Russia grew more powerful under her rule.

In the late nineteenth and early twentieth century, Ethiopian queen **Taytu Betul** fought against European colonialism, encouraged trade and modernized her country. She chose the site for Ethiopia's capital city, Addis Ababa, in 1866. When her husband became ill, Taytu Betul tried to gain more **political power** but was forced into retirement in 1910.

During World War Two, **Queen Wilhelmina** of the Netherlands became a symbol of resistance against German occupation. She made thirty-four wartime radio broadcasts from England – the Dutch people had to hide to listen to them in secret. When Wilhelmina returned home at the end of the war, people rejoiced and called her a **heroine**.

EMPRESS THEODORA

Powerful daughter of a bear-trainer

Born c. 497; died c. 548

Despite being the daughter of a bear-trainer and an actress, Empress Theodora became one of the most powerful women of the Byzantine Empire. And she was a champion of women's rights, too!

By the age of eighteen, Theodora was a successful actress, dancer and singer, travelling around northern Africa. Returning home to Constantinople (modern-day Istanbul, Turkey), she met the Byzantine emperor-to-be, Justinian. He was enchanted by her, but the emperor was not allowed to marry an actress, by law … so, he had the law changed and made Theodora his wife.

Justinian became emperor in 527. Theodora was Justinian's trusted adviser and met foreign envoys (representatives of countries), a responsibility usually kept for emperors alone. She was the first empress of the Eastern Roman Empire to have coins minted with her face and name on them.

Some of Justinian and Theodora's decisions as rulers proved unpopular – riots started and rampaging mobs set fire to Constantinople. Justinian's advisers urged him to flee but Theodora said he should stay and restore order. The church of Hagia Sophia had been burnt to the ground, so the couple funded an impressive rebuild. It became the largest building in the world.

Theodora's death in 548 left Justinian heartbroken. As a champion of women's rights, including divorce laws and safety for vulnerable women, Theodora did not forget her own humble beginnings, despite her rise to power.

CHAMPION OF WOMEN'S RIGHTS…

RUTHLESS RULERS

Queen Ranavalona I of Madagascar, who ruled from 1828 to 1861, was a ruthless tyrant! After her husband died, she killed all relatives who had a claim to the throne. It is thought that around half of Madagascar's people were killed under her **reign of terror**.

Queen Isabella of Castile and King Ferdinand of Aragon believed that all bad things in Spain were caused by the Jewish and Muslim people. They set up the Spanish Inquisition – an inhumane system that tried to force Muslims and Jews to convert to Christianity.

Native American **Bíawacheeitchish** (meaning 'Woman Chief') earned her name and reputation as a **fearless warrior** who bravely fought and killed many attackers. Fearless, she led her Crow tribe to raid another, the Blackfoot, in the mid-1800s. She killed many people, and took horses and scalps as trophies.

When **Mary I** inherited the throne of England in 1553, she restored the country to the Roman Catholic faith. Many found guilty of not practising Catholicism were burnt at the stake. Approximately 300 people died, earning her the nickname '**Bloody Mary**'.

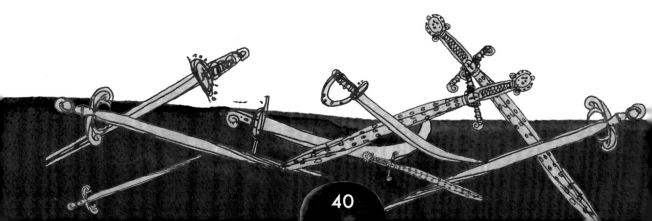

 Queen Amina was a ruthless sixteenth-century warrior queen of Zazzau (modern-day Nigeria). According to **legend**, she would marry a new husband after every battle, then have him executed the next morning!

 Queen Elizabeth I executed anyone who crossed her, including her cousin, **Mary, Queen of Scots**. As head of the Protestant Church of England, Elizabeth executed around 200 priests and their supporters.

 Sayyida al Hurra was a pirate queen of Tétouan (northern Morocco) in the early sixteenth century. She wanted to avenge the persecution of Muslims by Queen Isabella and King Ferdinand. She led the life of a **fierce pirate**, attacking Portuguese and Spanish ships, earning herself the nickname 'Queen of the Med'.

 The Celtic warrior queen **Boudicca** and her troops were said to be terrifying! They ransacked and burned down towns in their rebellion against the Roman Empire. The **fearsome army** is estimated to have killed over 70,000 people.

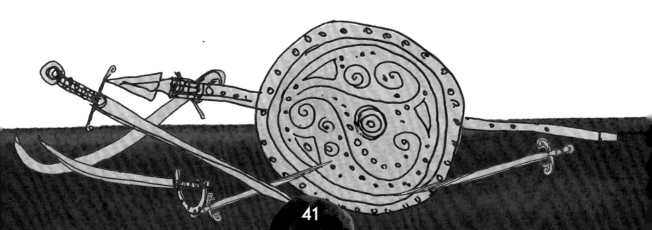

EMPRESS WU ZETIAN

Ruthless ruler of the Tang dynasty

Born 624; died 705

Wu Zetian, a ruler during the Tang dynasty, was the first and last empress of China to rule in her own right.

At the age of fourteen, Wu Zetian entered the court of Emperor Taizong as a servant. Upon his death she was sent away to a Buddhist convent. But Wu Zetian was unwilling to accept this fate, and with the help of the new emperor, Gaozong, she escaped from the convent back to the imperial court.

Ruthlessly ambitious, she had two sons and a daughter with Gaozong but the female child was found murdered. Wu Zetian accused Empress Wang, the emperor's wife, of the crime. Smitten with Wu Zetian, Gaozong believed her. Wu Zetian took her place at Gaozong's side … and had Empress Wang executed. Many scholars believe that Wu Zetian herself killed the child in order to get rid of the empress.

Because a woman couldn't present her face at court, Wu Zetian wielded power from behind a screen, although she still sat on a throne. It was well known that the emperor relied heavily on her, and when he died in 683, she remained in power, acting as dowager empress for their sons.

In 690, Wu Zetian took the ultimate step. She ordered the last of her sons to give up the throne so she could take power for herself. It wasn't until 705, when Wu Zetian was more than eighty years old, that she was finally made to yield power to her youngest son, Zhongzong.

During her reign, Wu Zetian enhanced the position of women and promoted the lower classes into government. Under Wu Zetian's rule, China began to accept music, arts and textiles from other cultures. But really, she was not so different from male emperors – Wu Zetian was a calculating murderer when anyone opposed her.

A CALCULATING MURDERER...

ROYAL RESIDENCES

The **palace of Alhambra** in Granada, Spain, became a Christian court in 1492 when **Queen Isabella** and King Ferdinand defeated the Muslim King Abu Abdallah Muhammad XII, known in Europe as Boabdil. 'Alhambra' – 'red' in Arabic – was so-called because of the reddish earth with which the outer walls were built.

Native American warrior chief **Bíawacheeitchish** would have lived in a **large tipi** made from bison skin and wooden poles.

In 1774, Louis XVI of France gave a set of keys glistening with many diamonds to his new bride, **Marie Antoinette**. They were for the **Petit Trianon**, a small chateau in the grounds of the Palace of Versailles. Marie Antoinette made it into her own little kingdom, where she could escape from the royal court with her friends.

Jhansi Fort in Uttar Pradesh, India, was the home of the warrior queen **Rani Lakshmibai**. According to legend, with her adopted son on her back, she jumped on horseback from the high fortress tower into the night to escape the British Army in 1858.

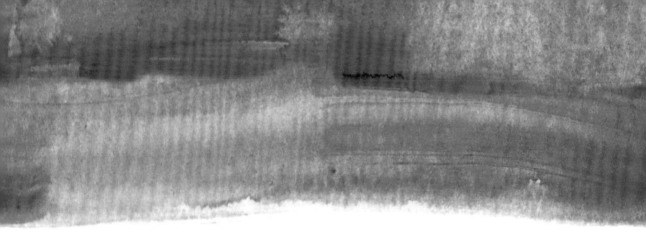

Empress Dowager Cixi lived in her **palace in the Forbidden City** in Beijing. Finished in 1420, it was built for the emperors of China. Whilst Cixi lived there, she had a beautiful wonderland of lakes, gardens and pavilions built.

The **Winter Palace** in St Petersburg, Russia, was the home of Russian tsars, including **Catherine the Great**. When she came to the throne in 1762, she began an impressive art collection to be housed there. After the Russian Revolution of 1917, the palace became part of the Hermitage Museum.

Queen Victoria was the first royal resident of London's **Buckingham Palace** in 1837. Today, if **Queen Elizabeth II** is residing at the palace, the Royal Standard flag is flown. If the Union Flag is seen flying, then the Queen is not there.

LADY K'ABEL

Supreme warrior of the Centipede Kingdom

Ruled between 672 and 692

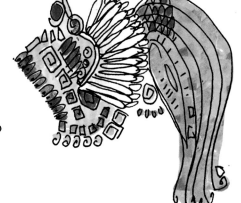

When the tomb of a great Maya warrior queen, Lady K'abel, was unearthed in the ancient city of El Perú-Waka, Guatemala, in 2012, it led to much excitement. The discovery of the Centipede Kingdom's female leader allowed archaeologists to learn more about the role of powerful women in Mayan society.

The Mayans were known for their impressive stone cities, monuments and pyramids, and for their hieroglyphic carvings. They were skilled mathematicians and astronomers who mapped out the stars. Respect and fear of nature and the elements formed the basis of their religion: Chaac with his lightning axe could bring on the rains; Kinich Ahau was god of the sun; and Kukulkan – a huge feathered serpent – flew up from his lake into the sky to produce much-needed water when the crops were dry. Mayan kings and queens spoke with their gods to protect the people from their enemies.

From decoding the hieroglyphic symbols in K'abel's tomb, archaeologists learned that the seventh-century warrior queen was married to King K'inich Bahlam II of the Wak (Centipede) Kingdom. Her high status was confirmed by the prestigious items found in the tomb, from jade jewellery to ceramic pots and stone figurines of gods.

K'abel's title of 'Kaloomte', or 'supreme warrior', gave her higher authority than the king, making her the most powerful person in the kingdom.

SEVENTH-CENTURY WARRIOR QUEEN...

STYLISH SOVEREIGNS

Some queens were very aware of their image and how they portrayed themselves to their public. Often the trendsetters of their day, what they wore would dictate a season's fashion.

Queen Elizabeth I's image was carefully designed to display **power and wealth**. Wide silk gowns were embroidered and covered in jewels. She wore a ruff – a high-frilled collar made of fine gauze that was put carefully over wires and starched. A small crown and jewels would complete the outfit.

Empress Dowager Cixi of China loved dressing up and having her photograph taken. Her embroidered blue silk gown below is decorated with chrysanthemums (signifying a long life), and **woven with pearls**, gold and jade. Her hair is in the style of '*Liangbatou*', where the hair is parted in two, supported with wire and decorated with ornaments.

In this image, **Cleopatra** wears a sheer white linen dress and leather sandals. Her gold necklace is encrusted with jewels of agate, topaz, amethyst and garnet. Her headpiece is a golden decorated vulture, which showed her to be an important queen.

Queen Christina Alexandra of Sweden is dressed here in a man's velvet robe, knee-length coat with decorative cuffs and pockets, breeches, leather shoes with a heel, and a wig.

Empress Elisabeth of Austria (also known as Sisi) was one of the most stylish women of her time. What she wore in court, everyone would rush to copy. The famous fashion designer Charles Worth designed her **ballgowns** – a corset and crinoline skirt would make the shape. In this image, she wears diamond stars in her hair and a white satin ballgown with décolleté neckline, which is overlaid with a star-decorated white satin tulle (a sheer fabric).

Marie Antoinette was known to love the fashion designer Rose Bertin. She had a workshop built for Rose in Versailles and made her '**Minister of Fashion**'. In this image, Marie Antoinette's '*robe à la française*' dress is made of silk. It is decorated with ribbons, lace frills, bows and tassels, and held up with a wide-hooped pannier frame. Silk heeled slippers and her famous bouffant hairdo complete the outfit.

QUEEN GUNNHILD
Triumphant mother of kings
Born c. 910; died c. 980

Gunnhild was an infamous Viking queen who made many enemies. She appears in long poems called sagas, but not everyone believes she was a real, historical figure. She was said to be the wife of the ruthless king Eric Bloodaxe. Their marriage had created a union between two families: the Norwegian Yngling and the early Danish monarchy.

The crown of Queen Sonja of Norway (born 1937).

When Harald Fairhair – the first Norwegian king – gave complete control of his lands to Eric, it sparked a brotherly feud resulting in the death of four of Eric's siblings. Eric continued to reign with terror and the ambitious Gunnhild was often seen to be the cause of this. News of the pair's tyranny reached the ears of Norwegian king-to-be, Haakon the Good, who sailed from England to challenge them.

Gunnhild and Eric fled to Orkney, Scotland, where he was accepted as king. They then moved to York, where he became king of northern England. In 954, Eric was killed in battle. When this news reached Gunnhild, life as she knew it ended: the people of England blamed her for the bloodshed that Eric had rained on them. Gunnhild eventually fled to Denmark.

Her son, Harald Greycloak, became King of Norway in 961 after winning a battle against King Haakon. Gunnhild returned triumphantly and became known as the Mother of Kings. But she met a gruesome end when her brother, Harald Bluetooth, had her drowned in a bog.

INFAMOUS VIKING QUEEN...

QUEENLY COSTUMES

Septimia Zenobia wore a long tunic with decorative cuffs, belted and embroidered in gold. The fabrics for the tunic and turban would have been **exquisite silks** and linens purchased from the caravans that travelled through Palmyra along the Silk Road.

Grand Empress Ujin Börte, wife of Genghis Khan, wore a crossed robe or tunic with a hat known as a **'boqta'**, which was worn by noblewomen. It was covered in silk and had peacock feathers on the top.

Empress Theodora wore a mantle cloak and a tunic decorated with jewels. Her crown was covered in precious gems.

Eleanor of Aquitaine wore a crown with a linen veil and barbette (a strap that goes under the chin), a mantle cloak, and a white linen embroidered dress with a leather and gold belt.

Queen Isabella of Castile wore a white skullcap, kerchief (fabric used to cover the head) and crown. Her silk gown was laced at the back with a split skirt and square neckline beautifully embroidered in gold thread. Slits in the sleeves allowed for a white shirt to be pulled through.

Margaret, Maid of Norway wore a crown, a dyed wool dress with ornamental backstitching along the seam and cord edging, a fur cloak, stockings and leather boots.

ELEANOR OF AQUITAINE

Mother of a Lionheart

Born 1122; died 1204

Eleanor of Aquitaine was one of the most powerful women of the Middle Ages. Her wealthy father's death set her at risk of kidnapping, so Eleanor was put in the care of Louis VI of France. He arranged Eleanor's marriage to his son, Louis VII. In 1137, Louis and Eleanor became king and queen.

But things soon began to fall apart. After Eleanor gave birth to a second daughter in 1151, Louis, disappointed at not having a son, ended their marriage.

Within two months Eleanor had sent word to Henry Plantagenet – the future King Henry II of England – to come to her. They were soon married. Louis VII was furious!

In 1154, Eleanor and Henry were declared king and queen of England. They had five sons and three daughters, and together built the powerful Plantagenet dynasty. But things began to fall apart for Eleanor again, and by 1168 she had returned to Aquitaine.

Five years later, Henry II's sons plotted against him, demanding a share of his rule, and the ambitious Eleanor sided with them, returning to England. The plot failed and although she tried to flee dressed as a man, Eleanor was captured. She was imprisoned for fifteen years until Henry II's death, when their son – King Richard I, the Lionheart – released her.

Richard the Lionheart spent most of his ten-year reign away on crusades, so Eleanor ruled in his name. She even raised ransom money and organized his release when he was held captive in Germany.

Eleanor died at the age of eighty-two. A determined and ambitious queen, she secured over three hundred years of rule for the Plantagenet dynasty.

A DETERMINED AND AMBITIOUS QUEEN...

ALL THE WORLD'S A STAGE

During the reign of **Queen Elizabeth I** of England, the arts and theatre grew significantly. William Shakespeare was writing plays and the Globe Theatre was built, but plays were also performed in Elizabeth's royal court. In the summer months, Elizabeth loved to tour the country visiting nobility, and they would put on plays with extravagant scenery and costumes. Elizabeth had her own theatrical group called **Queen Elizabeth's Men**, but women were not allowed on stage, so female parts, like Juliet in *Romeo and Juliet*, would be played by young boys.

French queen **Marie Antoinette** had a small theatre built near the Palace of Versailles. The decoration inside was made of **papier-mâché**, painted in cream, blue and gold to resemble a full-sized grand theatre.

The current queen of Denmark, **Margrethe II**, is a devoted fan of ballet. Her love of the arts has inspired her creatively, and she has worked as a costume and set **designer** for ballet and film.

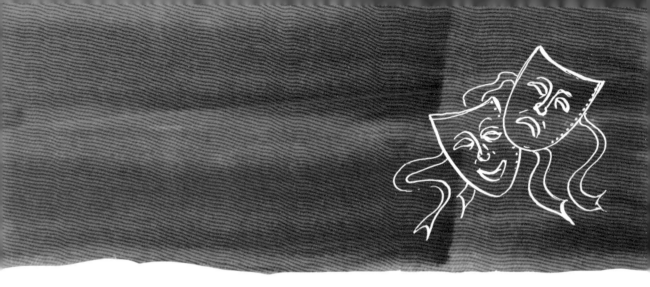

 Empress Dowager Cixi was known to watch Chinese opera at the **Pavilion of Pleasant Sounds** (Changyin Pavilion) inside the Forbidden City in Beijing. Still standing today, the pavilion is nearly twenty-one metres (over seventy feet) tall and has three floors: the Stage of Happiness, the Stage of Wealth and the Stage of Longevity.

 **Theodora**, the powerful sixth-century Byzantine empress, was born into a family of performers and herself acted, sang and danced. The **Hippodrome** was mainly used for chariot racing, and actors, acrobats, musicians and animal trainers would entertain the crowds during the intervals.

 When **Queen Eleanor of Aquitaine** governed Poitiers, France, it is said that she established the **Court of Love**, which attracted poets and artists, promoting the ideas of chivalry, honour and knightly respect for women. Poets and singers known as troubadours would perform songs about legends and stories, such as that of King Arthur and his Knights of the Round Table.

QUEEN TAMAR

Saintly monarch of Georgia

Born 1166; died 1213

Tamar was born to Georgian monarchs, King George III and Queen Burdukhan. The king proclaimed that he would share the throne with his daughter from the day she turned twelve. Father and daughter reigned together for five years.

After King George III's death in 1184, Tamar was recognized as sole ruler. This was the first time a woman had ruled Georgia and many of the nobles were not happy about it. They were particularly anxious to find her a husband, so that she might have an heir to the throne and the future would be more certain.

A husband was soon found for Tamar – a Russian prince called Yuri. But the match was unhappy and within two years they were divorced – a rare event for the time. Tamar married again but to her own choice – Prince David of Alania. Together they had two children, both of whom ruled Georgia in time.

Georgia's location at the crossroads between Europe and Asia made it vulnerable to attack. Queen Tamar successfully defended her Christian kingdom from neighbouring Muslim countries. A true politician, she made inspiring speeches that rallied her troops to fight for their country, believing they were on God's mission. In this way she expanded her kingdom and came to rule large areas of Azerbaijan and Armenia.

Georgia thrived during Tamar's rule. When she suddenly died, she was greatly mourned, and made a saint by the Georgian Orthodox Church.

A TRUE POLITICIAN...

GODS, GODDESSES AND RELIGION

Cleopatra worshipped Isis, a powerful and protective goddess said to have magical powers. Being a mother made Isis a role model for women, and as **Mother of Egypt**, Cleopatra identified with her.

Boudicca, the Celtic warrior queen, would have followed Druidism, believing in many gods and goddesses and the importance of nature. It is thought the Celts also believed in **reincarnation** – that when someone dies, their soul comes back in another form. The Romans feared that this gave the Celts more courage when going into battle.

During **Empress Wu Zetian**'s rule, China became very cosmopolitan. Wu Zetian was fascinated by **Buddhism**, which was practised in India and Tibet. Buddhism allowed her to rule as a woman. Through her, Chinese Buddhism became very popular.

Believing it contained a splinter of the cross of Christ, **Queen Tamar** of Georgia bought a pendant known as the '**True Cross**'. She used it before military campaigns, and had her nobles kneel before her to kiss the pendant, in the hope it would bring them victory.

Marie Antoinette of France and **Tsarina Alexandra Feodorovna** of Russia both believed in the **divine right** of kings (and queens!) – that God had given them the right to rule. They refused to recognize that the people were angry and pushing for change, which led to both their downfalls.

Being a member of the Native American Crow tribe, **Bíawacheeitchish** would have practised spiritual rituals through ceremonies of, prayer, art and song, including the **Sun Dance** ceremony. The belief was that all things in nature were sacred and that through these customs they could connect with the natural world.

MARGARET, MAID OF NORWAY

Scotland's lost queen

Born 1283; died 1290

Margaret, Maid of Norway, was only seven years old when she was sent abroad to claim the title of Queen of Scotland. Her mother's father, Alexander III of Scotland, had died just before her fourth birthday, and as the only remaining heir, she had inherited the title.

Margaret was to be met on her arrival by Edward of Carnarvon, the son of King Edward I of England. Although he was even younger than Margaret, they were to be married to unite the two realms.

With her future mapped out, Margaret left home on a ship bound for Scotland. Sadly, she never arrived. At sea, Margaret became very sick and a storm blew the ship off course. Tragically, while the ship docked in Orkney, an island north of Scotland, the young queen died.

Without a marriage to unite the country with England, Scotland was thrown into crisis. With the true heir – Queen Margaret – dead, thirteen different competitors wasted no time in fighting for the throne.

Historians today question whether Margaret should be called queen as she was never officially crowned. What isn't called into question is the true tragedy of this sad tale.

A FUTURE MAPPED OUT...

QUEEN ISABELLA OF CASTILE
Powerful Spanish monarch
Born 1451; died 1504

At two years old, Isabella was third in line to the throne and not destined to be queen, yet she found herself contending for rule of the Spanish kingdom of Castile.

Isabella's older brother, King Henry, had tried to marry her to Alfonso V of Portugal. But Isabella knew that there she would find herself a powerless queen consort. So, she rebelled and made a secret proposal of marriage to Ferdinand, heir to the neighbouring kingdom of Aragon, who would allow her to keep power in Castile.

In 1469, Isabella travelled to meet Ferdinand, who joined her disguised as a servant. Within four days they were married, but as second cousins they needed approval from the Pope. This was denied, but they went ahead anyway, waiting months before finally receiving the Pope's blessing.

Hearing that Isabella had defied him, a furious Henry attempted to deny her the throne in favour of his daughter Joanna. Upon his death, Isabella quickly pronounced herself queen, prompting a war that ended in 1479 with Joanna's defeat.

Isabella and Ferdinand were determined to unite Spain under their Catholic Christian rule. In 1492, having defeated King Boabdil in Granada, the 700-year Muslim presence in Spain came to an end. Boabdil's request that Muslims be free to practise their religion was accepted but soon ignored, and conversion to Christianity was enforced. Under the infamous Spanish Inquisition, both Jews and Muslims were forced to convert on pain of death.

Queen Isabella died in November 1504. A powerful and influential queen, she championed education, exploration and the arts. She set up Spain as a new superpower and with her military success was highly respected in what had previously been a man's world.

NOT DESTINED TO BE QUEEN...

QUEENS ON THE MOVE

Queen Elizabeth I would travel around England on horseback visits known as '**progresses**', aimed at keeping up her good public image. Travelling was difficult as the roads were poor, but the queen was well entertained by nobles who wished her to favour them.

Empress Dowager Cixi had a small railway built in the gardens of her palace. It ran from her private residence to the dining hall. The **carriages** had different coloured curtains: Cixi's were yellow, the colour reserved only for the emperor.

During World War Two, **Queen Elizabeth II** joined the Women's Auxiliary Territorial Service, and trained as a **mechanic** and truck driver. She is the only person in the United Kingdom allowed to drive without a driving licence!

Legend says that the **Queen of Sheba** travelled to meet King Solomon by camel caravan, bearing silks, spices, gold and **precious stones**. Camels were used as transport because they could travel for a long distance without water.

Queen Victoria was the first British monarch to travel by train but not the first queen! **Queen Adelaide**, wife of William IV, travelled by train in 1840, two years before Queen Victoria.

It is said that **Cleopatra** made a dramatic entrance to meet Julius Caesar. She was rolled up in a carpet and carried to the emperor. Her surprise introduction must have **intrigued** him. They went on to have a son together.

Both **Boudicca** and **Septimia Zenobia** showed prowess by leading their armies into battle while standing in **chariots** pulled by horses.

ISABELLA AND HER DAUGHTERS

**Joanna of Castile
1479–1555**

**Isabella of Aragon
1470–1498**

**Queen Isabella
of Castile
1451–1504**

**Maria of Aragon
1482–1517**

**Catherine of
Aragon
1485–1536**

GRACE O'MALLEY

Pirate queen of Ireland

Born *c.* 1451; died *c.* 1504

Grace O'Malley was a sixteenth-century pirate queen who fought for her rights and ruled the waves off the west coast of Ireland.

The O'Malleys were a great seafaring family and Grace was a determined young girl, hungry for adventure on the open water. When her father told her she couldn't join him on an expedition because her long hair would catch in the ship's ropes, Grace didn't take no for an answer and cut her hair short.

When her father died, Grace became the queen and fearless leader of her clan. At the height of her power, she had hundreds of men and many ships at her disposal.

Grace was married twice and bore four children during her life. According to legend, she gave birth to her third child on the high seas during a trading expedition to the Mediterranean. Only a few hours after the birth of her baby, Grace picked up a gun and joined a fight on deck with a group of Algerian pirates who had invaded her ship.

Hearing of Grace's pirating exploits, the English governor in Ireland, Sir Richard Bingham, made it his mission to capture her. He had her locked up in gaol, where she narrowly escaped the death penalty. On her release, Grace discovered she had been left penniless as English power in Ireland had increased while she was in prison. Her sons and brother had attacked Bingham in retaliation and also been imprisoned.

A furious Grace wanted her property back, as well as the freedom of her sons and brother. In 1594, she set sail for England to meet Queen Elizabeth I.

At the historic meeting, Grace and Elizabeth spoke in Latin as neither spoke the other's language. Grace refused to bow to Elizabeth – some say because she was a queen herself and some because she refused to recognize Elizabeth as Queen of Ireland. Bingham was ordered to return the stolen land and release the prisoners – on the condition that Grace supported the queen. The courageous Grace went on to live a secure life under the queen's patronage.

SHE RULED THE WAVES!

WIVES OF HENRY VIII

First: Catherine of Aragon, Divorced 1485–1536

Third: Jane Seymour, Died 1508–1537

Fifth: Catherine Howard, Beheaded 1523–1542

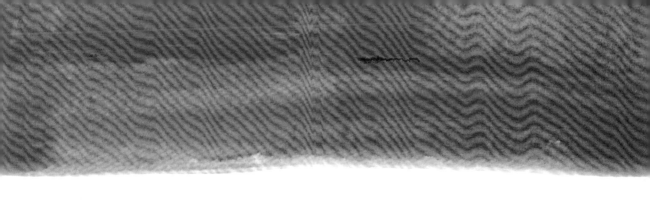

Fourth: Anne
of Cleves,
Divorced
1515–1557

Second: Anne Boleyn,
Beheaded
1501–1536

Sixth: Catherine Parr,
Survived
1512–1548

NOBLE NIBBLES

In 1889, the queen consort of Italy, **Margherita of Savoy**, visited Naples with King Umberto I. A chef created a pizza in the colours of the Italian flag – red, white and green – using tomato sauce, mozzarella and basil, and named it in her honour: '**Pizza Margherita**'.

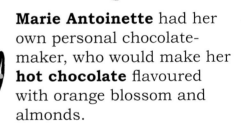

Marie Antoinette had her own personal chocolate-maker, who would make her **hot chocolate** flavoured with orange blossom and almonds.

The first **gingerbread men** are said to have been invented as entertainment for the court of **Queen Elizabeth I**. They were moulded into shapes and decorated to look like important people.

Queen Elizabeth I was so fond of 'marchpane' – which we now know as **marzipan** – that her frequent nibbling led to her teeth being cracked and black at the end of her life. For royal feasts, marchpan was moulded into wonderful shapes and used as table decorations that could be eaten as dessert.

Empress Cixi of China had her own kitchens in the Forbidden Palace. Here, delicious delicacies were made. She would have over a **hundred dishes** cooked each day, but would only eat a tiny bit from each plate. Perhaps she was afraid of being poisoned, but in any case a tiny bit of a hundred dishes would still be a lot of food!

Cleopatra was said to have bet Mark Antony that she could spend more money on a meal than him. She had a servant bring her a **bowl of vinegar**, unclasped her precious pearl earring and dropped it into the bowl. Once the pearl had dissolved in the vinegar, she drank it and won the bet.

On **Queen Victoria**'s Golden Jubilee, servants were selected from India to come and work at the celebration. One of those chosen was Abdul Karim, who one day served the queen with a **curry** that she reported in her diary was 'excellent'. It was probably not the first time she had eaten curry, but perhaps this version was nearer to a true Indian dish. From then on, this curry was on the menu at Buckingham Palace at least twice a week.

QUEEN ELIZABETH I

Good Queen Bess

Born 1533; died 1603

King Henry VIII had longed for a son and heir. He already had a daughter, Mary, by his first wife. When Elizabeth was born, Henry's disappointment with her mother, Anne Boleyn, would ultimately lead to Anne's execution, paving the way for a third wife to provide a son.

That wife was Jane Seymour, who gave birth to a baby named Edward. When Henry VIII died in 1547, nine-year-old Edward came to the throne, but his death from a fever at the age of fifteen meant the throne was once more up for grabs.

There were many arguments over who should rule, and when her half-sister Mary became queen, Elizabeth was imprisoned for a year in the Tower of London. Later, when Mary died, Elizabeth became queen. She was twenty-five years old.

When Elizabeth was crowned, England was in religious upheaval. Mary had made England a Catholic country, so Elizabeth changed it back to Protestant – the faith of her father, Henry VIII. She named herself Supreme Governor of the Church of England.

Elizabeth was not married, and this worried the English parliament – no husband or heir could mean instability for the country. Attempts were made to find her a husband, but for one reason or another they came to nothing. Elizabeth made a virtue of her single state, claiming that England was her husband and its subjects her children.

In 1587, her ministers convinced Elizabeth that her cousin Mary, Queen of Scots, was plotting against her. Elizabeth had her beheaded. The following year, Philip II of Spain launched an Armada of 130 ships to invade England, but they were defeated in foul weather by Elizabeth's navy, led by Sir Francis Drake.

The first Elizabethan era is often thought of as a golden age, where arts, exploration and literature blossomed.

ENGLAND WAS HER HUSBAND...

NORTH AMERICA

EUROPE

AFRICA

SOUTH AMERICA

THE NEW WORLD

It is vital to acknowledge the role that European queens played in the slave trade. In 1492, **Queen Isabella of Castile** gave Christopher Columbus her approval and funding to sail west to the Indies. He was searching for a new route to lands already discovered but instead found lands that Europeans did not know existed, with potential for untapped riches and space for new settlements.

As the newly discovered Caribbean and Americas opened up, more and more human labour was needed to work the land of what Europeans called the New World. Slavery was not unknown in the Old World. The capture, sale and transportation of African people to work on the plantations, where crops such as sugar and tobacco were produced, seemed the answer to the shortage of workers. Packed into slave ships like animals, the treatment of these people was brutal, and many died en route.

Queen Elizabeth I approved Captain John Hawkins' first slavery expedition in 1562. On this journey, he captured around 300 Africans, transported them across the Atlantic Ocean and exchanged them for goods. Elizabeth was pleased with the profits that the African slave trade promised, and supplied further vessels for Hawkins' voyages. The seeds of the British Empire had been sown.

The trans-Atlantic slave trade continued to supply Caribbean and American plantations with human labour. Known as the 'trade triangle', slave traders would first leave the European ports and sail to West Africa. There they would buy people and load them into ships. The horrendous journey to America and the Caribbean across the Atlantic – known as the 'Middle Passage' – took six to eight weeks. Anyone who survived would be sold and put to work. The ships then returned to Europe with goods that the enslaved people had farmed, such as sugar, tobacco, cotton and coffee.

It is estimated that 12.5 million Africans were transported across the Atlantic Ocean as slaves. This human cost was something that was ignored for centuries, in favour of profit and exotic produce.

QUEEN NZINGA

Formidable African ruler

Born c. 1581; died 1663

Queen Nzinga of Ndongo and Matamba – modern-day Angola – fought against Portuguese forces that attempted to control the region in order to increase their profits from the slave trade. She was a fearless warrior and politician.

Growing up, Nzinga fought the Portuguese alongside her father, the King of Ndongo. But when he died in 1617, Nzinga's brother seized power and appointed himself king. He was eager to protect his throne and feared Nzinga and her heirs, so he had her only son murdered. Nzinga was heartbroken.

Nzinga's brother was a weak ruler and needed the Portuguese-speaking Nzinga's help to negotiate an agreement with the conquering force. Faced with the ruin of her beloved country, Nzinga agreed to help her cruel brother.

The Portuguese set up a meeting and arranged it so they would sit on chairs, with Nzinga seated on a floor mat, allowing them to hold the advantage and talk down to her. But the quick-thinking Nzinga asked her maid to become a human chair and sat on the maid's back. This gave Nzinga eye contact and equal footing with the Portuguese governor. Nzinga negotiated an agreement that protected her homeland from the Portuguese troops. However, they did not respect the new treaty for long and re-invaded Ndongo.

When her brother died in 1624, Nzinga became queen. She fled with her people to escape the invasion, conquering the neighbouring kingdom of Matamba as she went.

The defiant queen continued to fight the Portuguese. Eventually, they gave up and recognized Ndongo and Matamba as an important country that should be negotiated with as equals.

Queen Nzinga ruled for nearly forty years, leaving behind her a land that had become a sanctuary for escaped slaves.

AN ASTUTE POLITICIAN...

THE TWO ELIZABETHS

Queen Elizabeth I

1533–1603

Motto: *Semper Eadem*

('Always the same')

Queen Elizabeth II
1926–present
Motto: *Dieu et mon droit*
('God and my right')

QUEEN CHRISTINA ALEXANDRA

Rebellious 'King' of Sweden

Born 1626; died 1689

From a young age, Queen Christina Alexandra of Sweden fought against the traditional idea of what a girl should be. Her father encouraged this by educating her as if she were a prince. After inheriting the crown when her father died, Christina became Queen of Sweden – but the title she inherited was 'king'.

Christina loved books, music, philosophy and science, and attracted many scientists and scholars to Stockholm. After reigning for nearly twenty-two years, she gave up her throne (known as 'abdication') in 1654.

Within days, Christina slipped out of Sweden into Denmark, disguised as a man. As an ex-queen of Sweden, she was not safe riding through Denmark – the two countries were long-standing enemies. She settled in Rome as a guest of Pope Alexander VII, where she converted to Catholicism.

Christina tried unsuccessfully to become Queen of Naples and went to Paris to convince the French to take her side. However, she was shunned by French society, which was not used to a woman dressing like a man. After several failed attempts to get the French on board, she returned to Rome where she lived out her final years.

Christina challenged society by defying the norm. She influenced European culture and was known as one of the most educated women of her time. Tolerant of others and their views, she lived her life with rebellious spirit. Christina was buried at St Peter's Basilica in the Vatican City, Rome – a most unusual honour for a woman.

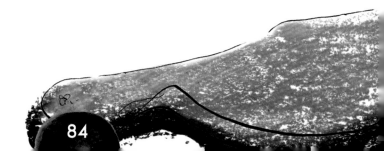

GRUESOME ENDINGS

Mary, Queen of Scots was found guilty of plotting to kill her cousin **Queen Elizabeth I**. Following Mary's execution in 1587, her dog, a Skye terrier, was found hiding under her dress and refused to leave. The loyal companion was taken away and pined for its mistress, dying shortly after.

In 1793, **Marie Antoinette** of France was convicted of high treason and executed by **guillotine**. Her last recorded words were, "Pardon me, sir, I did not do it on purpose." She had accidentally stepped on her executioner's foot.

Anne Boleyn, the second wife of England's King Henry VIII, was tried and convicted of high treason in 1536. She was imprisoned in the Tower of London, then taken to be executed by the Hangman of Calais – a man with a reputation for being skilled at beheading by wielding a sword. **Catherine Howard**, Henry's fifth wife, met a similar fate just six years later, although in her case it was an axe, not a sword, that ended her life.

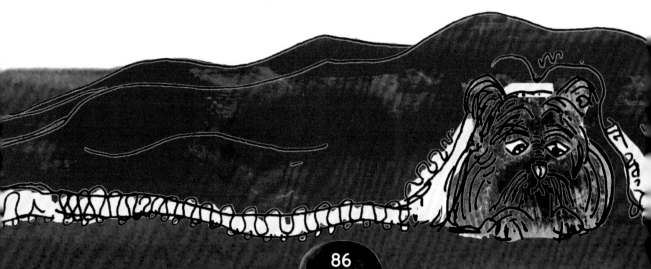

 Queens **Cleopatra** and **Boudicca** were both defeated by the Romans. Rather than be publicly humiliated, it is thought that they took their own lives.

 Empress Elisabeth of Austria, also known as Sisi, had her life tragically cut short when she was assassinated in Geneva in 1898. She had been taking a walk when an Italian anti-monarchist man stabbed her in the heart.

 From 1236 to 1240, **Razia Sultana** reigned over Delhi, the first Muslim female ever to do so. She wore men's clothes and called herself '**Queen of the Times**'. However, the nobles were not happy and wanted Razia Sultana's brother, Muizuddin Bahram, on the throne. He led an army against her and Razia was captured and killed.

QUEEN NANNY
Courageous Jamaican heroine
Born c. 1686; died c. 1755

In seventeenth-century Jamaica there lived a group of people known as the Maroons. They were descendants of West Africans who had been transported to work as slaves on the European sugar plantations of Jamaica. Some spent their lives imprisoned, but others managed to escape to live in the safety of the Blue Mountains. One was to become a fearless chief: Queen Nanny.

Nanny was born in the 1680s in Asante, now known as Ghana, Africa. After being captured and transported across the Atlantic Ocean, she and her brothers were sold on to work in the plantations.

Queen Nanny managed to escape and formed a small village called Nanny Town, high up in the Blue Mountains, far away from the European land owners. She became a folk hero who courageously led raids against the Europeans and set free a thousand slaves, who joined her in Nanny Town. She taught her people how to become warriors by camouflaging themselves with leaves and branches and hiding in the trees, so when the enemy attacked they would be bewildered, thinking the trees had come alive.

The Maroons lived as farmers and hunters but all the while were anxious that the plantation owners wanted to destroy the life they had carved out for themselves. Queen Nanny's mountain home offered a safe hideaway that was difficult to attack. After a period of unsuccessful British military raids, land was finally given to them and they were able to live their lives freely.

Her death remains a mystery, whether at the hands of the British in 1755, or living to an old age in Nanny Town. Today, the Maroons still take pride in their resistance against slavery. Through songs and legends, the memory of Queen Nanny is alive within the community.

Queen Nanny was made a national hero in Jamaica in 1976, the first woman to be awarded the honour.

A FEARLESS CHIEF...

MARIA THERESA
Energetic empress and mother
Born 1717; died 1780

Maria Theresa was born to Holy Roman Emperor Charles VI and Elizabeth of Brunswick. Having lost their only son, the couple named Maria Theresa heir to their many lands in central Europe – the Habsburg Empire – including Austria, Hungary and Croatia.

On Charles's death in 1740, some countries within the empire disputed Maria Theresa's right to rule as a woman. This led to the War of the Austrian Succession, which lasted until 1748 and involved most of the major powers of Europe. Maria Theresa was eventually crowned Queen of Hungary and over time successfully defended her right to rule the entire empire.

In 1736, Maria Theresa married Francis Stephen, Duke of Lorraine, making him co-ruler. However, she viewed herself as the true ruler and tried to keep him away from political decisions. Together they had sixteen children! Maria Theresa viewed the children as political assets, marrying them off into royal families around Europe in order to strengthen the Habsburg Empire. One of her daughters, Marie Antoinette, became Queen of France.

Under her rule, Maria Theresa united and improved the Habsburg state, which had been left bankrupt by her father. She was determined to modernize the empire and changes were made in agriculture, the military and education.

A devout Roman Catholic, Maria Theresa was religiously intolerant – Jews and Protestants were targeted and often banished. Books that questioned the Catholic faith were not accepted.

The unexpected death of her husband in 1765 devastated Maria Theresa. She announced that her son, Joseph II, would rule with her and she retreated from public life, wearing black for the rest of her days.

MOTHER OF MARIE ANTOINETTE...

CLEOPATRA ON FILM

The 1963 Hollywood movie *Cleopatra* was one of the most expensive films ever made. From the start, it had many setbacks.

Filming began in Pinewood Studios, England. Due to the British winter being very different to the hot Egyptian climate, it soon became a problem. It was so cold that you could see the actors' breath whenever they spoke! The leading actress, Elizabeth Taylor, soon became very ill. Accepting defeat, the whole production had to move to Italy at great expense.

The costume budget was huge and Elizabeth Taylor had around sixty-five costume changes. Her wigs cost thousands of dollars because they were made of real human hair and woven with gold beads.

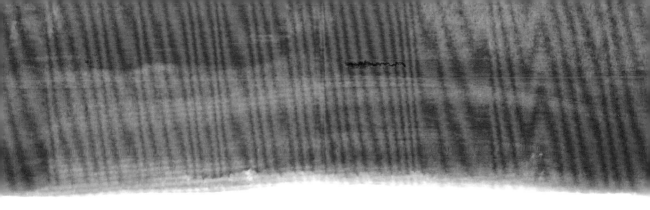

Cleopatra's large floating barge and palm trees were flown in from the USA. Constructing the extravagant sets caused shortages of building materials and builders across Italy.

The crew even faced unforeseen issues on location. The beach chosen for a battle scene still had live mines from the Second World War – the area had to be cleared and made safe, adding more money to the already spiralling costs.

Cleopatra's entrance scene involved thousands of extras, taking a lot of time and money to film. When the crew reviewed the footage at the end of the day, they realized there was a man on camera selling ice creams. As the film was made before special effects were available for use, they had to go back and reshoot the whole scene!

CATHERINE THE GREAT

Ambitious empress of Russia

Born 1729; died 1796

Catherine was born as Sophie Friederike Auguste von Anhalt-Zerbst, to a German prince. At fifteen, she travelled to Russia to meet her husband, Peter III. Catherine learned the Russian language and changed her name from Sophie upon joining the Russian Orthodox Church.

The marriage took place in 1745, and had been arranged to strengthen the relationship between Russia and Germany. It was not a happy marriage. Peter and Catherine had very little in common with each other.

In 1762, Peter became Emperor of Russia. Only months later, he was captured by Count Orlov, the brother of one of Catherine's lovers, and died mysteriously while being held prisoner. There is no hard evidence linking Catherine to his death, but it certainly fitted in well with her plans. Catherine now found herself Empress of Russia.

Catherine's ambition as empress was to make Russia more like the rest of Europe. She embraced science and culture, and had a vast art collection. She wanted to educate the entire Russian population, including the 'serfs' (the working class). The nobility resisted this move, refusing to give their permission for the serfs to attend school.

Catherine enjoyed conflict and fought wars with the mighty Ottoman Empire over land. Under her rule, Russia increased its borders, and new towns and cities were built.

During her reign, Catherine transformed Russia into one of the great powers of Europe – a golden age in Russian history.

SHE ENJOYED CONFLICT...

QUEEN MARIE ANTOINETTE
The last queen of France
Born 1755; died 1793

The daughter of Empress Maria Theresa of Austria (see page 90), Marie Antoinette was just fourteen when she was sent to marry the heir of the French throne.

As she crossed the French border to meet her husband-to-be for the first time, Marie Antoinette had to change into French gowns and was made to say goodbye to her ladies-in-waiting and her dog, Mops. This parting was so painful that she demanded Mops be brought to her in Paris as soon as possible.

Despite leaving behind everything to do with Austria, Marie Antoinette was seen as an outsider and the French people did not warm to her. When King Louis XV died in 1774, his son became Louis XVI and Marie Antoinette became queen, but this did not improve her public image. Her lavish wardrobe and the wealth displayed at court was in great contrast to the food shortages and high taxes experienced by the poor.

From 1789, the unimaginable happened: in what came to be known as the French Revolution, power was stripped from the aristocracy. Marie Antoinette and Louis XVI were placed under house arrest. They attempted to escape, disguised as servants, but instead of following advice to travel in two light carriages, the queen insisted on keeping the family together in a large, heavy carriage. The king and queen were recognized when they stopped at Varennes and they were arrested all over again.

As the French Revolution progressed , Louis XVI was put on trial. Marie Antoinette boldly defended the monarchy and the rights of her children. In September 1792, the monarchy was abolished and in January of the following year, Louis was executed.

On 16 October 1793, Marie Antoinette was convicted of high treason and sent to the guillotine. Over a thousand years of a ruling French monarchy had come to an abrupt and gruesome end.

AN OUTSIDER...

THE UNDERWEAR OF MARIE ANTOINETTE

Chemise of embroidered linen.

Corsets and undergarments were needed to make sure Marie Antoinette's *robe à la française* gown kept its shape.

Firstly, a linen knee-length chemise was worn under a corset. A lady-in-waiting would help to lace up the corset over the chemise, which was pulled in tight to create a narrow silhouette. A pannier made of iron, leather and tied with canvas ties would be put on around the waist. A floor-length petticoat would go over the top of the pannier and a decorative underskirt. The robe was parted in the middle in a V-shape so the underskirt could be seen.

Corset made from embroidered damask and stiffened with stitched-in whale bones.

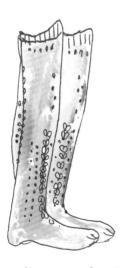

Silk or linen embroidered stockings.

A silk garter tied to hold up the stockings.

BÍAWACHEEITCHISH
Woman Chief of the Crow people
Born c. 1806; died 1854

Bíawacheeitchish (meaning 'woman chief') was a Native American chief. Born into the Gros Ventres tribe, she was captured as a young girl by a warrior from the neighbouring Crow tribe who had lost his own sons. He adopted Bíawacheeitchish and taught her many skills, including marksmanship.

When her adoptive father died, Bíawacheeitchish hunted buffalo instead of sitting with the other women. She was allowed to go on the warpath with the men against another tribe and gained a reputation for being a fearless warrior.

Within the Crow tribe, Bíawacheeitchish was highly respected and given a position of honour that many male warriors never achieved. She was described as being 'two-spirit', meaning that she mixed both male and female traits.

Bíawacheeitchish went on to become an important leader and rose to be a high-ranking member of the council of chiefs – a position no other woman had ever reached. She also married several wives, which increased her wealth and prestige. Through this role, she was involved in many peace negotiations with the native tribes of Missouri, USA.

After several years of peace, in a cruel twist of fate, she was shot and killed in a surprise attack by a member of the Gros Ventres, her birth tribe.

A FEARLESS
WARRIOR...

THE
BRITISH
EMPIRE
IN
1901

THE BRITISH EMPIRE

The first twenty years of **Queen Victoria**'s rule (from 1837) saw Great Britain claim new land across the world. By 1858, after the First War of Indian Independence the year before, the East India Company, which had ruled India for over a hundred years, ended its control. The British Crown took over, with Queen Victoria named **Empress of India** in 1877. India became known as 'the jewel in her crown'.

The prime minster at the time, Benjamin Disraeli, was keen to expand Britain's empire even further. He believed it would make Britain richer, and that bringing British customs and Christianity to people of other countries was a positive thing to do.

So, the 'scramble for Africa' began. European nations, including France, Germany, Belgium, Italy, Portugal and Spain, as well as Britain, raced against each other to conquer Africa and gain its riches of gold, diamonds and minerals. These nations divided up Africa and marked out their territories, giving no thought to how this affected the people that lived there.

When Victoria's Golden Jubilee celebrated her fifty years on the throne in 1887, she gave a feast with over fifty foreign kings, queens and dignitaries from Britain's colonies. By the end of Victoria's reign in 1901, Britain had control of a quarter of the globe and ruled over 400 million people. The British people saw their queen as Britannia ruling the waves, as the popular song said.

But the reality was that many British colonies did not want to be ruled by another country. They wanted their independence. Outbreaks of war, as well as peaceful demonstrations, became more and more common.

Victoria did not live to see her empire break up. It was not until after the Second World War ended in 1945, that independence for most British colonies began to become reality. An organization called the Commonwealth of Nations, usually known as the Commonwealth, originally formed in 1926 and is now made up of fifty-four independent countries who wanted to continue a relationship with Great Britain and with each other.

QUEEN VICTORIA

Grandmother of Europe

Born 1819; died 1901

Princess Alexandrina Victoria of Kent's childhood was unhappy. Her protective mother forced her to spend hours learning, and she had no siblings or friends to play with. After the death of her uncle, King William IV in 1837, Alexandrina inherited the throne in 1837 aged just eighteen. She became Queen Victoria.

In 1838, people lined the streets of London cheering, "Long Live the Queen!" for Victoria's coronation. Two years later, Victoria married her German cousin, Prince Albert of Saxe-Coburg and Gotha. They went on to have nine children.

By the end of William IV's reign the monarchy had become unpopular, so Victoria and Albert visited towns and cities across Britain to improve their image. They supported many charities to win favour amongst the people. Between 1840 and 1882, Victoria survived eight assassination attempts, earning her even greater admiration.

In 1861, Albert died of typhoid. A heartbroken Victoria went into mourning for many years, wearing black for the rest of her life. Victoria and Albert's nine children gave her a total of forty grandchildren. Eight of these sat on the thrones of Europe, earning Victoria the nickname 'grandmother of Europe'.

Victoria's sixty-three-year reign saw extraordinary changes. Abroad, the British Empire expanded greatly. At home, by the turn of the twentieth century, British life had changed forever as people moved from villages into towns for work. For the first time, workers had seaside holidays as new railways allowed people to travel to the coast. Children's lives improved as many more went to school, and women's campaigns for the right to vote gained pace – even though Victoria opposed them!

At the time of her death, Victoria was the longest reigning British monarch ever – surpassed only recently by her great-great-granddaughter, Queen Elizabeth II.

COLOUR CHART
EMPIRE
REST OF THE WORLD
SEA

THE ROYAL SHOE

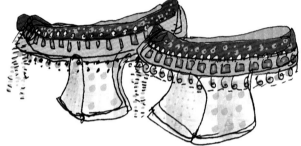

Empress Dowager Cixi's platform shoes with a wooden base, made from appliqué, silk, satin, cotton and beads.

Catherine de' Medici was said to be less than 1.5 m (5 ft) tall. She had a shoemaker create a pair of shoes with a heel for her wedding, to make her taller. This shoe was different to the platform shoe already in use. It instantly became fashionable – Catherine had started a fashion for heeled shoes that still exists today.

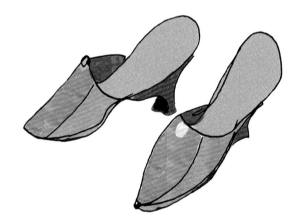

Catherine the Great's shoes, made from silk brocade cotton and embroidery.

Marie Antoinette's silk slipper with a leather sole and wooden heel.

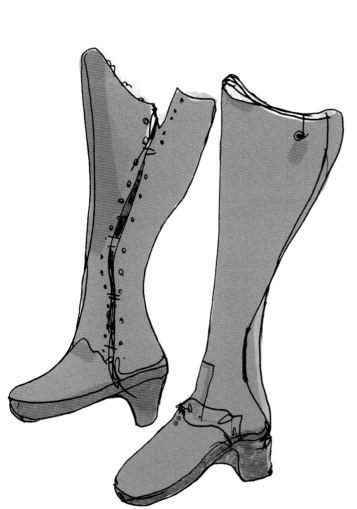

Queen Elizabeth I's knee-length lace-up riding boots made of leather or cloth.

Native American chief **Bíawacheeitchish** would have worn a moccasin shoe made of deerskin, decorated with beads.

RANI LAKSHMIBAI
Indian warrior queen
Born 1835; died 1858

Rani (Queen) Lakshmibai was born to a wealthy family and named Manikarnika Tambe. Unlike most girls growing up in India at the time, even wealthy ones, she learned fencing, shooting and horse riding as well as reading and writing.

When she was still young, Manikarnika was married to the maharajah (king) of the Indian state of Jhansi and given the name of Lakshmibai. They had a son but he died at only a few months old. The maharajah was himself dying, so he adopted a son in order to gain an heir and to protect the state of Jhansi from being given away to the British East India Company.

But when the maharajah died in 1853, the British refused to acknowledge the adopted child as an heir and seized Jhansi.

In 1857, an uprising broke out in the Indian military town of Meerut. Rebels protesting against the treatment of Indian soldiers by the British marched to Delhi and then on towards Jhansi. As she had refused to give up Jhansi to the British, Lakshmibai became a leading figure of this Indian rebellion.

Some British officials and their families had taken refuge in Lakshmibai's fort. They were promised they would not be harmed as they left, if they left their weapons behind. But as they exited the fort, they were all killed. The horrified British blamed Lakshmibai for allowing this, as she had signed an oath saying she would protect them. There are many different opinions about whether Lakshmibai was involved in any way in the massacre or was herself a victim of impossible circumstances.

In retaliation, the British military surrounded Lakshmibai's fort. Her army fought on, and after a fierce battle many were left dead. Lakshmibai escaped to the city-fortress of Gwalior, continuing the fight against the British. The Indian warrior queen, who dressed as a man in battle, was later killed in combat.

CROWN JEWELS

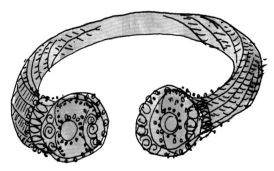

Tribal leaders of Celtish clans would wear a neck ring called a 'torc' to symbolize power and wealth. **Boudicca** would likely have worn one similar to this.

Rani Lakshimibai was said to wear a pearl necklace and bangles when going into battle against the British.

Queen Elizabeth I wore a diamond, gold and mother-of-pearl ring that was taken from her body when she died in 1603. No one then knew that the ring contained a secret portrait of her mother, Anne Boleyn, as Elizabeth never spoke of her.

The legendary Briolette of India is rumoured to be one of the oldest diamonds in history. **Eleanor of Aquitaine** is said to have brought it to England. Her son, the English king Richard the Lionheart, took it on the Third Crusade. It was not seen again until the sixteenth century when King Henry II gave it to his mistress.

Marie Antoinette was falsely accused of being involved in a diamond necklace swindle. Although innocent, the French people did not believe her and she fell further from grace.

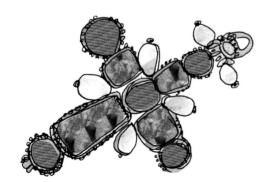

Queen Tamar's 'True Cross' pendant (see page 60).

Catherine the Great had a gold and blue enamel ring made with a miniature portrait of her favourite dog.

EMPRESS DOWAGER CIXI
Ruthless Chinese ruler
Born 1835; died 1901

Little is known of the early life of Chinese Empress Dowager Cixi. Originally named Yi, it is thought her parents presented her to the court of the Xiangfeng Emperor, Yizhu, at the age of sixteen. Here she befriended Empress Zhen, the emperor's first wife. She was soon noticed by Yizhu and gave birth to his only son, Tongzhi, in 1856.

Yizhu died in 1861. He had arranged that eight elders would rule together until Tongzhi became emperor. Realizing this to be a good moment to seize power, Yi, with the help of Empress Zhen and two of the late emperor's brothers, staged a *coup d'état* to remove the elders.

The coup was successful and the path clear for the women to rule as empress dowagers until Tongzhi came of age. At this point both women changed their names – Yi became Cixi, and Zhen became Ci'an.

In 1873, when Tongzhi came of age, he became emperor. But he died two years later, leaving no heir. So, acting swiftly, the scheming Cixi adopted her young nephew, Guangxu, and put him on the throne, in order to retain rule for herself and Ci'an.

When Ci'an died in 1881, Cixi was left as sole empress and ruled alone for eight years. She had to step down when Guangxu came of age and took on the role of emperor. He tried to make changes that Cixi and her advisers instantly opposed. This resulted in another coup, with Guangxu put under house arrest. He was allowed to be emperor, but in name only. Once again, the plotting Empress Dowager Cixi ruled alone.

Ruthless to the end, Empress Dowager Cixi named her two-year-old great-nephew as her heir, after allegedly poisoning Emperor Guangxu the day before she died.

A PLOTTING EMPRESS...

MAGNIFICENT MARRIAGES

Cleopatra wed her younger brother, Ptolemy XIII, to become co-ruler with him. Then when he died, she married her other brother, Ptolemy XIV! Siblings were encouraged to marry so that the royal **bloodline** would remain pure.

It was said that when **Queen Min of Korea** married King Gojong, the wig she wore was so heavy that a servant had to stand behind to support it!

Queen Victoria started the tradition of wearing a **white wedding dress**. Before, brides had just worn their best dress. Victoria's outfit had a 5.5 metre (18 feet) train, and she wore a wreath of orange blossoms on her head. The wedding cake weighed around 136 kg (300 lbs) and was decorated with figures of the happy couple dressed in ancient Greek costumes.

On 16 May 1770, the prince who would become Louis XVI of France married **Marie Antoinette**. The celebrations continued for two weeks until a tragic firework accident on the Place de la Concorde in Paris killed 132 people. It was seen as a **bad omen** for their future together.

When Prince Abdullah of Jordan married **Rania**, who became his queen, the multi-tiered cake was huge – luckily the ceremonial sword used to cut it was long enough to reach!

Queen Elizabeth II married Prince Philip of Greece and Denmark in 1947, when she was still Princess Elizabeth. Britain was recovering from the Second World War, so she had to collect coupons to buy fabric to make her dress, just like other wartime brides. Food was still being rationed in 1947, so the wedding cake ingredients had to be sourced from around the world. This earned the cake the name '**The 10,000 Mile Cake**' – it was 2.7 metres (9 feet) high and had four tiers!

QUEEN LILIUOKALANI [lee-lee-oo-oh-kah-lah-nee]

First queen of Hawaii

Born 1838; died 1917

Queen Liliuokalani was Hawaii's first queen – but last ever monarch.

Born in 1838, Liliuokalani was named heir to the throne after her brother's death. She married the son of an American sea captain and they adopted three children together. Just a few months after she was crowned in 1891, her husband died.

Liliuokalani opposed American businesses that wanted more control of Hawaii for sugar and pineapple planting. Her brother had signed an agreement allowing American settlers more voting rights. When Liliuokalani came to power she wanted to reverse this, taking power back for the Hawaiian monarchy and people.

In 1893, a coup was staged – backed by the US government – which overthrew Liliuokalani, forcing her to give up her role of queen. Two years later, the authorities discovered weapons buried in her garden. Accused of attempting to reinstate the monarchy, Liliuokalani was arrested and charged with treason.

Despite her denials, she was found to be guilty, fined a sum of money and sentenced to five years' hard labour. This sentence was reduced to house arrest and confinement to one room in the royal palace. After a year, Liliuokalani was returned to her home where she lived twelve more months under house arrest.

Liliuokalani was a talented songwriter who composed over 160 songs or *meles* (Hawaiian chants). The most famous of these is 'Aloha 'Oe', which she originally wrote about a farewell embrace between a young couple. 'Aloha 'Oe' is a cultural symbol of Hawaii and is still sung to this very day.

A TALENTED SONGWRITER...

PALACE PETS

Catherine the Great loved an opera based on the Beauty and the Beast story so much that she named her **greyhound** Zemira after the heroine. Zemira slept with Catherine in a cradle next to her bed. When Zemira died, Catherine had a large tombstone etched with the words '**Beloved dog of the Great Queen**'.

On her eighteenth birthday, **Queen Elizabeth II** was given her first **corgi**, Susan. She was so attached that Susan went along on the royal honeymoon! With a lifelong love for the breed, the queen has since had more than thirty corgis.

Empress Dowager Cixi of China kept many dogs, her favourite being the **Pekingese**. She had bamboo dog houses made and they each had silk jackets embroidered with gold thread.

SUSAN

ZEMIRA.

The seventeenth-century king and queen of England, William of Orange and **Mary II**, loved their **pug dogs** and would tie orange ribbons into bows around their collars. William's great-grandfather – William I, Prince of Orange – was apparently saved from assassination by his pug!

When Christopher Columbus returned from his voyages across the Atlantic, he brought **Queen Isabella of Castile** many gifts, including colourful parrots.

Marie Antoinette loved the countryside. When the Palace of Versailles became too much, she would hide away with friends in a **miniature village** she had built. There was a farm with cows, pigs and chickens, a working windmill and a dairy!

Queen Elizabeth II has been given many animals as gifts, including tortoises, sloths, bears, beavers and an elephant from Cameroon named Jumbo. They were all homed at London Zoo.

YAA ASANTEWAA

Courageous African leader

Born c. 1840; died 1921

Yaa Asantewaa was a heroine of the Ashanti Empire (now in modern-day Ghana).

She led a rebellion against British colonialists who were expanding into Ashanti territory. The king, Prempeh I, had refused to meet British demands. Eventually, the British toppled his government and exiled him to the Seychelles.

The British governor, Frederick Hodgson, demanded in the name of Queen Victoria that the Ashanti people hand over the 'Golden Stool' – their sacred throne – so that he could assume power over the nation. The chiefs were outraged but disorganized, so the courageous Yaa Asantewaa stepped in and told them that if the men would not go forward, then she would call upon the women.

Yaa Asantewaa was made war-leader, the first and only female in this role in the Ashanti history. She gathered an army of over 5,000 to fight against the British. After months of battle, General Hodgson called for a ceasefire. The Ashanti agreed, but only if their demands were met, which included the release of King Prempeh I. The British refused and poured more troops into the area to outnumber the Ashanti, who were captured and killed in large numbers.

In 1900, Yaa Asantewaa was also exiled to the Seychelles. She died there twenty years later, having never returned home nor seen King Prempeh I restored to his throne.

The Ashanti finally gained their freedom from the British in 1957, as part of Ghana. The Golden Stool remains in their hands to this day.

THE ONLY FEMALE WAR-LEADER...

GRAND HOBBIES

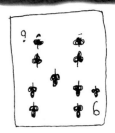

Rani Lakshmibai, was reported to enjoy lifting weights and **wrestling** before she'd even had breakfast! She also liked fencing, horse-riding, archery and teaching her servants self-defence.

Marie Antoinette was known to play chess as well as the harpsichord to pass the time.

The ancient Egyptians liked to play board games. In a wall frieze, **Queen Nefertiti** can be seen playing 'senet'. This was played on a long board painted with thirty squares, where knuckle bones and sticks were thrown to move pieces along.

Many queens enjoyed writing as a hobby. **Queen Victoria** kept a journal, and **Empress Elisabeth of Austria** and **Taytu Betul** of Ethiopia wrote poetry. **Queen Rania of Jordan** has written children's books, including one called *The Sandwich Swap*, about tolerance and friendship across boundaries.

Queen Isabella of Castile was the inspiration for the queen piece in a **chess** set. The rules of chess changed in the late fifteenth century when Isabella was one of the most powerful women in Europe.

Queen Elizabeth II keeps racing pigeons and is president of the Royal Pigeon Racing Association. She owns around two hundred birds.

Eleanor of Aquitaine, **Catherine the Great** and **Elizabeth I** all enjoyed **falconry** – the hunting of wild animals by a trained bird of prey.

The Italian queen **Margherita of Savoy** was a keen **mountaineer**. She climbed Punta Gnifetti, a peak in the Alps on the border between Italy and Switzerland, to visit the **Margherita Hut**, a mountain hut named after her.

QUEEN MIN OF KOREA

The ambitious Empress Myeongseong

Born 1851; died 1895

Queen Min married King Gojong of Korea at sixteen. The king's father, the Daewongun ('prince of the great court'), hoped Min would be a traditional wife who hosted tea parties and gossiped, but she preferred to read books and study. The Daewongun and Queen Min did not get on, and when her new-born son died, she accused the Daewongun of poisoning him. They became sworn enemies.

In 1873, Queen Min helped to plot against the Daewongun, so that King Gojong could rule directly. The Daewongun was removed as acting regent and exiled from court. Queen Min was now queen consort, ruling alongside her husband.

Within a year of King Gojong and Queen Min's direct rule, Japan tried to take control of land in Korea. At first, King Gojong resisted the Japanese, but he finally signed an agreement with them.

A worried Queen Min began to modernize the Korean army. The military encouraged the Korean people to riot against the Japanese. But this uprising caused the king and queen to be removed from their palace. Min's enemy, the Daewongun, was reinstated.

Korea was under Chinese protection so Queen Min appealed to China for help. They sent in troops who arrested the Daewongun, charging him with treason. But the Chinese were defeated and made to sign an agreement declaring that they had no interest in Korea. Desperate, Min turned to Russia, angering the Japanese again. On 8 October 1895, a group of assassins stormed the royal palace. They seized King Gojong, and on finding Queen Min, killed her and her assistants.

In 1902, Gojong, now emperor, gave Queen Min the posthumous title of 'Empress Myeongseong'. The Japanese rule of Korea continued until 1945, when Japan surrendered to the Allied forces at the end of the Second World War.

ASSERTIVE AND AMBITIOUS...

QUEENLY COSTUMES

It is said that **Rani Lakshmibai** went to battle in a red cotton or muslin sari, which she would fold into her belt to create a loose trouser called a **'soldier's tuck'**. She was also said to wear her pearl necklace and gold anklets.

Catherine the Great's blue and white military dress was trimmed with **gold braid** to represent her cavalry regiments. She would likely have worn the outfit shown here for a military parade or event.

Queen Min wore a '*hwarot*', the traditional dress for Korean royal women in the Joseon dynasty.

Bíawacheeitchish would have worn a simple dress decorated with **elk teeth**, with leggings and moccasins. To keep warm she would have wrapped herself in deer or buffalo skins.

Alexandra Feodorovna once wore a ballgown made of silk gauze, satin, Chantilly lace and glitter.

TSARINA ALEXANDRA FEODOROVNA
The funeral bride
Born 1872; died 1918

A granddaughter of British Queen Victoria, Princess Alix of Hesse and by Rhine married Tsar Nicholas II of Russia in 1894, shortly after the death of Nicholas's father, Alexander III. Alix was given the name Alexandra Feodorovna when she joined the Russian Orthodox Church before her wedding. Due to Alexander III's recent death, she became known as the 'funeral bride'. Alexandra's arrival so soon after a death was seen as a bad omen by the Russian people, who mistook her shy manner for coldness.

At first, the Russian people celebrated the new Tsar Nicholas II. But then, at a celebration in Moscow, a stampede occurred, killing over a thousand people. On the same night, Alexandra and Nicholas were due to attend an extravagant gala. Acting on bad advice, they went. This infuriated the Russian people, who saw this event as unfeeling and another bad omen for the reign of Tsar Nicholas II and Alexandra.

Alexandra did not find her life or Russian customs easy. Her son Alexei, born after four daughters, suffered from haemophilia, meaning his blood would not clot. The smallest accident could cause him to bleed internally and give him dreadful pain.

A man who claimed to be a healer, a monk called Rasputin, entered the life of the vulnerable Alexandra. Her desperate search for a cure for Alexei meant that Alexandra relied heavily on Rasputin, and his political power increased. Rasputin's presence in the royal household angered the people of Russia. Calls to have Rasputin removed were ignored by the family, and eventually a group of nobles had him murdered.

The outbreak of the First World War in 1914 marked the beginning of the end for the Russian monarchy. Slaughter on a massive scale meant that an army who did not have enough food or bullets left their freezing trenches and went home to change the world. When the 1917 Russian Revolution began, Alexandra, Nicholas and their children, were arrested and imprisoned. They were all executed in July 1918.

Alexandra was the last tsarina of Russia, and in 2000 was named a saint – Saint Alexandra the Passion Bearer – in the Russian Orthodox Church.

Empress Matilda

In 1141, after escaping once before by hiding in a coffin, Empress Matilda (daughter of King Henry I of England) daringly escaped her prison a second time. She was lowered from the castle walls on a rope. Dressed in a white cloak, she ran for miles, crossing a frozen river to freedom.

Queen Elizabeth I

In 1554, Elizabeth I was imprisoned in the Tower of London after being accused of plotting against her sister, Mary I. She entered through Traitors' Gate – this was terrifying for her as it was where her mother, **Anne Boleyn**, had walked before being beheaded!

Queen Nanny

Before she was Queen Nanny of Jamaica, Nanny had been captured and transported across the Atlantic Ocean, and sold into slavery.

Marie Antoinette
In 1793, after months in prison, Marie Antoinette was put on trial, found guilty of treason and sentenced to death by guillotine.

Queen Liliuokalani
Accused of attempting to reinstate the monarchy, Liliuokalani was arrested and charged with treason.

CONVICTS OF THE CROWN

QUEEN ELIZABETH II
Longest-reigning British monarch
Born 1926

As third in line to the throne at birth, Princess Elizabeth was not destined to be queen. But her uncle's abdication and her father's death brought her to the throne in 1952.

Her coronation in 1953 was the first in the world to be televised. Those lucky enough to own a television invited groups of neighbours to watch the ceremony. Street parties were held across the country to celebrate the new queen. This was a big step forward in Britain's recovery from the Second World War.

In 1947, the then Princess Elizabeth had married Prince Philip of Greece and Denmark. They had four children, including the current heir to the throne, Prince Charles.

The queen celebrates two birthdays: her real one in April and an official one in June, which marks her coronation and is celebrated by the event Trooping of the Colour, where the queen is saluted by guards dressed in red tunics and bearskin hats. At this event in 1981, a man rushed at the queen's horse with a pistol and fired six shots – but she held her nerve and kept the horse under control.

Fifteen prime ministers have served during Queen Elizabeth II's reign. She has seen joyous and terrible events from the celebrations of the 1977 Silver Jubilee to the sudden death of Princess Diana and the fire at Windsor Castle. Queen Elizabeth II is the only living head of state to have served in the Second World War – at the age of eighteen she trained as a mechanic and truck driver.

As head of state for Great Britain, and as head of the Commonwealth, Queen Elizabeth II remains a strong and active figurehead.

SERVED IN THE SECOND WORLD WAR...

FANCY FUNERALS

 When **Queen Elizabeth I** died in 1603, the country mourned. People lined the streets of London to see her body carried in a hearse drawn by horses swathed in **black velvet**.

 A careful search of the woods was ordered by King Gojong of Korea after the horrific assassination of his wife, **Queen Min**, whose body had been burned. All that could be found was a bone from her finger. There was a large public funeral with thousands of lanterns, and giant wooden horses to carry her in the **afterlife**.

 When **Queen Victoria** died in 1901, she had written very specific instruction for her funeral. She was to be buried wearing her wedding veil and with a number of **mementos** of friends and family, including her husband's dressing gown and a plaster cast of his hand, as well as a lock of hair from her personal attendant John Brown and his picture.

 When **Empress Himiko** of Japan died in the third century, a large burial mound is said to have been made for her. The legend says that a hundred male and female attendants were **sacrificed** to be buried with her.

 Chinese **Empress Dowager Cixi**'s funeral was extravagant, and included the burning of a giant wooden boat covered in silk. The grand **ceremony** was believed to give the empress a better afterlife.

**The Queen
of Sheba**

Tenth Century BC

Cleopatra

Born *c.* 965 BC;
died *c.* 931 BC

Boudicca

Born *c.* AD 30;
died *c.* AD 61

**Empress
Jingū**

Born *c.* AD 170;
died *c.* AD 269

**Septimia
Zenobia**

Born *c.* AD 240;
died *c.* AD 274

**Queen
Tamar**

Born 1166;
died 1213

**Margaret, Maid
of Norway**

Born 1283;
died 1290

**Queen
Isabella**

Born 1451;
died 1504

**Grace
O'Malley**

Born 1533;
died 1603

**Queen
Elizabeth I**

Born 1533;
died 1603

**Marie
Antoinette**

Born 1755;
died 1793

Bíawacheeitchish

Born *c.* 1806;
died 1854

**Queen
Victoria**

Born 1819;
died 1901

**Rani
Lakshmibai**

Born 1835;
died 1858

**Empress
Dowager Cixi**

Born 1835;
died 1901

Empress Theodora

Born *c.* 497;
Died *c.* 548

Empress Wu Zetian

Born 624;
died 705

Lady K'Abel

Ruled between 672 and 692

Queen Gunnhild

Born *c.* 910;
died *c.* 980

Eleanor of Aquitaine

Born 1122;
died 1204

Queen Nzinga

Born *c.* 1581;
died 1663

Queen Christina Alexandra

Born 1626;
died 1689

Queen Nanny

Born *c.* 1686;
died *c.* 1755

Maria Theresa

Born 1717;
died 1780

Catherine the Great

Born 1729;
died 1796

Queen iliuokalani

3orn 1838;
died 1917

Yaa Asantewaa

Born *c.* 1840;
died 1921

Queen Min

Born 1851;
died 1895

Tsarina Alexandra Feodorovna

Born 1872;
died 1918

Queen Elizabeth II

Born 1926

1. The Queen of Sheba
2. Cleopatra
3. Boudicca
4. Empress Jingū
5. Septimia Zenobia

6. Empress Theodora
7. Empress Wu Zetian
8. Lady K'abel
9. Queen Gunnhild
10. Eleanor of Aquitaine

11. Queen Tamar
12. Margaret, Maid of Norway
13. Queen Isabella of Castile
14. Grace O'Malley
15. Queen Elizabeth I

22.

26.

18.

8.

N
W   E
S

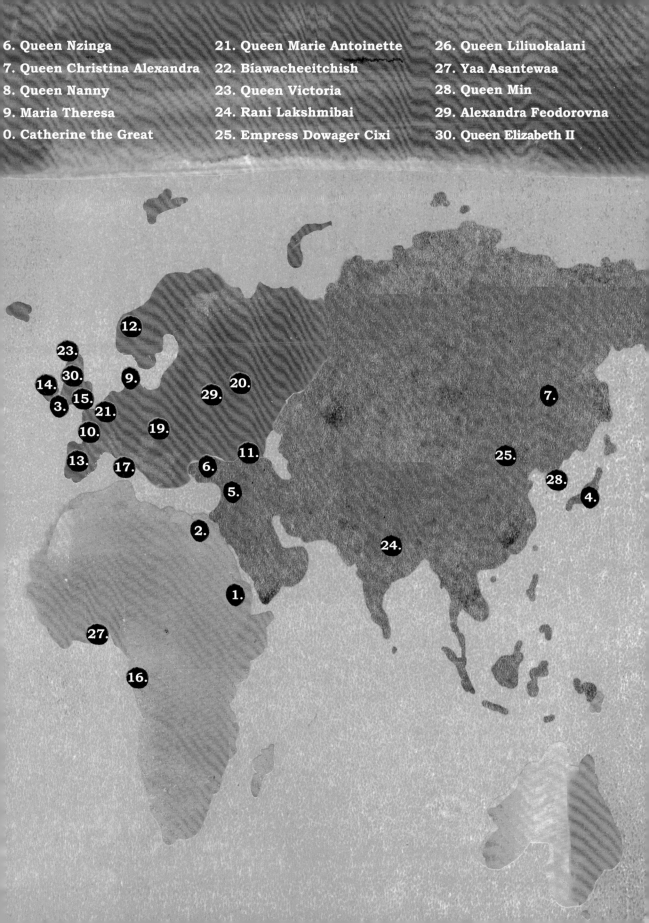

6. Queen Nzinga
7. Queen Christina Alexandra
8. Queen Nanny
9. Maria Theresa
0. Catherine the Great

21. Queen Marie Antoinette
22. Bíawacheeitchish
23. Queen Victoria
24. Rani Lakshmibai
25. Empress Dowager Cixi

26. Queen Liliuokalani
27. Yaa Asantewaa
28. Queen Min
29. Alexandra Feodorovna
30. Queen Elizabeth II

GLOSSARY

abdication
The act of stepping down from something, especially a king giving up the throne. When a king – or another person in power – gives up their position, they abdicate.

Allied forces
The victorious allied nations of World War One and Two, including Britain, France, Italy, Russia and the United States.

Anglo-Saxon
People from Germany and Scandinavia who came in ships across the North Sea to Britain during the fifth century. There were three main peoples: the Saxons, the Angles and the Jutes.

aristocrat
A member of the ruling class, usually those with nobility, money or both.

Asante Empire
Controlled what is now Ghana in the eighteenth and nineteenth centuries.

ballgown
A type of evening gown worn to a ball or a formal event. Traditionally it has a full skirt and fitted bodice.

British Empire
Comprised of Britain, the 'mother country', the colonies and other territories which were controlled by the United Kingdom. At the height of its power, the empire made up nearly one-quarter of the world's land surface and more than one-quarter of its population.

Byzantine Empire
When the Roman Empire split into two separate empires, the Eastern Roman Empire became known as the Byzantine Empire, which ruled most of eastern and southern Europe throughout the Middle Ages.

camel caravan
A series of camels carrying passengers and goods. Camels were used as transport because they could travel for a long distance without water and could withstand the harsh desert conditions.

Catholic
A Christian who is a member of the Roman Catholic religion. The Roman Catholic Church is led by the pope.

client state
A country which is controlled or depends on another larger, more powerful country for support and protection.

colony
A group of people from one country who build a settlement in another territory, or land. The practice of setting up colonies is called colonialism.

commoner
A person who is not privileged and holds no title or rank.

The Commonwealth
An organization of fifty-four independent nations who were once part of the British Empire.

cosmopolitan
A place of sophistication with the influence of many different countries and cultures.

coup d'état
The sudden overthrow of a monarch or government, usually done by a small group of people who then replace those in power.

The Crusades
A series of religious wars, during the Middle Ages, fought between Christians and Muslims over control of the Holy Land.

Silver Jubilee
A celebration held in the twenty-fifth year of a monarch's reign.

dynasty
The era during which one royal family rules a country or region over a long period of time.

Early Dynastic Period
Began when Lower and Upper Egypt were joined together as one country in c. 3150 BC. The main features of ancient Egyptian civilization, such as art, architecture and religion, took shape during this time.

Eastern territories
The Eastern Roman Empire which became the Byzantine Empire.

exile
When a person is forced to leave his or her country for political reasons or sometimes because they have committed a crime.

The East India Company
An English company formed for the exploitation of trade with East and Southeast Asia and India.

First War of Indian Independence
The unsuccessful rebellion against British rule in India in 1857–59.

Golden Age
An expression that people use when they are talking or writing about a period of great happiness, prosperity and achievement.

Golden jubilee
A celebration held in the fiftieth year of a monarch's reign.

Habsburg Empire
Habsburg was a family of dukes, kings and monarchs who expanded their empire through both war and marriage to other royal families. They ruled many lands in central Europe including Austria and Hungary for more than 600 years.

high treason
The crime of disloyalty to the Crown.

maharajah
The male ruler of an Indian state.

mele
A Hawaiian chant, song or poem, typically in praise of a leader or to commemorate a significant event.

Middle Ages
The period in European history that came between ancient and modern times. It lasted from c. AD 500–1500.

Mughal Empire
Ruled most of India and Pakistan in the sixteenth and seventeenth centuries.

nemes
The striped headcloth worn by pharaohs in ancient Egypt.

New World
The name given to the Americas and nearby islands. The name started in the early sixteenth century, shortly after America was discovered.

nobility
Members of high social class and rank.

Old World
Before the discovery of the Americas, people of the Middle Ages thought the world was only Europe, Asia and Africa. These continents are called the Old World.

Ottoman Empire
Ruled a large portion of the Middle East and Eastern Europe for over 600 years. It first formed in 1299 and finally dissolved in 1923, becoming the country of Turkey.

patronage
The support, encouragement and often financial aid given by a person.

Persian Empire
Included areas of modern-day Iran, Egypt, Turkey, and parts of Afghanistan and Pakistan. The Persian Empire lasted from c. 559–331 BC.

pharaoh
A ruler of ancient Egypt.

Plantagenet dynasty
A royal dynasty that ruled England for 331 years, from 1154 to 1485.

plantation
Farmed lands controlled by European settlers. Slaves worked on these plantations under incredibly harsh conditions.

Protestant
A Christian who belongs to the branch of the Christian church that separated from the Catholic church in the sixteenth century.

Qing dynasty
China's last great empire, ruling over the country from 1644 until it ended in 1912.

Roman Empire
The largest empire of the ancient world. The Roman Empire covered much of Europe, north Africa and the Middle East, lasting from 27 BC to AD 476.

Russian Revolution
Took place in 1917 when the peasants and working-class people of Russia revolted against the government of Tsar Nicholas II.

saga
A long story of heroic achievement.

serf
A member of the working class who worked on the land and had to obey the person who owned that land.

Tang dynasty
Ruled Ancient China from 618 to 907. This time period is sometimes referred to as the Golden Age of Ancient China.

Ten Commandments
The rules for life that God gave to Moses on Mount Sinai.

treason
The crime of betraying your country.

tyranny
A government in which a single person rules absolutely and in a cruel way.

War of the Austrian Succession
A war that involved most of Europe over the issue of Maria Theresa's succession to the Habsburg monarchy. The conflict lasted from 1740–1748.

PLACES TO VISIT

In 1851, The Great Exhibition took place in London. It was the first in a series of popular world fairs. Many people travelled to admire the new technology, arts and manufacturing on display. The fair was organized by Queen Victoria's husband, Prince Albert, and with the money made from the fair, they built colleges and museums, including the Science Museum, Victoria and Albert Museum and Natural History Museum, all of which you can still visit today in London.

Here are some museums and other heritage sites around the world that you can visit in person or online to find out more about the queens in this book.

EUROPE

The Louvre
The Louvre and its collections house art from the West and a number of ancient civilizations, from the Middle Ages to 1848.
www.louvre.fr/en

The Museum of Cultural History
A part of the University of Oslo, including the Historical Museum and the Viking Ship Museum.
www.khm.uio.no/english

The Palace of Versailles
The principal royal residence of France from 1682 until 1789.
www.en.chateauversailles.fr

Rijksmuseum
The national museum of the Netherlands.
www.rijksmuseum.nl/en

Schönbrunn Palace
The imperial summer residence of the Habsburg dynasty.
www.schoenbrunn.at/en

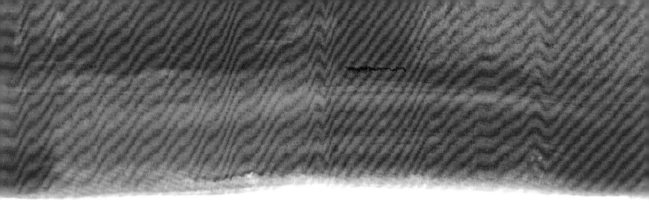

RUSSIA

The State Hermitage Museum
This collection includes over 3 million works of art and world culture artefacts.
www.hermitagemuseum.org

UNITED KINGDOM

Ashmolean Museum
The University of Oxford's museum of art and archaeology.
www.ashmolean.org

Balmoral Castle
The Scottish holiday home to the British Royal Family.
www.balmoralcastle.com

The British Museum
A museum covering all fields of human knowledge.
www.britishmuseum.org

Colchester Castle
A museum showcasing history from Celtic Kings, through Roman invasion and Boudiccan revolt, to Norman conquest and medieval life.
www.colchester.cimuseums.org.uk/visit/colchester-castle

Hatfield House
The childhood home of Queen Elizabeth I.
www.hatfield-house.co.uk

Hever Castle
The childhood home of Anne Boleyn, second wife of King Henry VIII.
www.hevercastle.co.uk

Historical Royal Palaces
The charity that looks after the Tower of London, Hampton Court Palace, the Banqueting House, Kensington Palace, Kew Palace and Hillsborough Castle.
www.hrp.org.uk

International Slavery Museum
A museum dedicated to increasing the understanding of all forms of enslavement.
www.liverpoolmuseums.org.uk/international-slavery-museum

Osborne House
Queen Victoria's seaside retreat.
www.english-heritage.org.uk/visit/places/osborne

Royal Collection Trust
The Royal Palaces, Residences and Art Collection of the British monarchy.
www.rct.uk

Royal Museums Greenwich

A group of sites dedicated to enriching people's understanding of the sea, the exploration of space, and Britain's role in world history.
www.rmg.co.uk

Victoria and Albert Museum

The world's leading museum of art and design.
www.vam.ac.uk

UNITED STATES

Iolani Palace

The official residence of Hawaii's monarchy.
www.iolanipalace.org

The Metropolitan Museum of Art

A museum with over 5,000 years of art from around the world.
www.metmuseum.org

National Gallery of Art

A collection that spans the history of Western art.
www.nga.gov

National Museum of African American History and Culture

A museum devoted to the documentation of African American life, history and culture. Part of the Smithsonian Institution.
www.nmaahc.si.edu

National Museum of the American Indian

The world's most expansive collection of Native artefacts. Part of the Smithsonian Institution.
www.americanindian.si.edu

Rosicrucian Egyptian Museum

The largest collection of Egyptian artefacts on exhibit in western North America.
www.egyptianmuseum.org

Smithsonian Institution

The world's largest museum, education and research complex.
www.si.edu

INDEX

ABOUT THE AUTHOR

Victoria Crossman worked in film costume for a number of years on projects ranging from the *Harry Potter* and *Star Wars* film series, to *Finding Neverland* and *Captain Corelli's Mandolin*. In 2019, she completed a Master's degree in Children's Book Illustration. Her work is heavily influenced by her background in costume, both from the research perspective and the embracing of detail, colour and pattern.

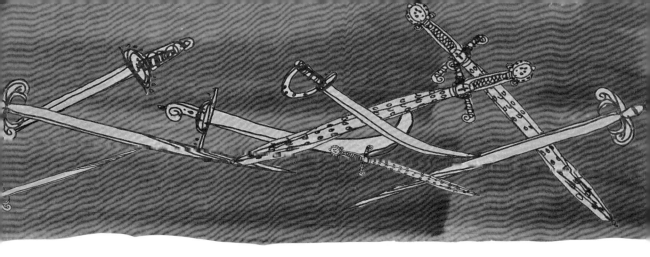

ACKNOWLEDGEMENTS

To Dave, Poppy and Evelyn, my loving supportive family. Without you, I never would have believed that I could produce a book of which I am immensely proud.

Iain Clark, I am indebted to you for the hours of support and gentle guidance that you have given me, thank you.

Mum, Dad and Charlotte – who taught me that anything is possible. Angela Marin, Clive Cunningham and Pam – thank you.

Thank you to my agent, Lauren Gardner, who had faith in me and was as enthusiastic as I was about *Queens*. And at Scholastic, my fantastic editors, Elizabeth Scoggins and Leah James, and designer Bleddyn Sion – I hope that we can be proud of what we have produced together.

Lastly, to all the queens – whose inspirational stories I have been honoured to share.

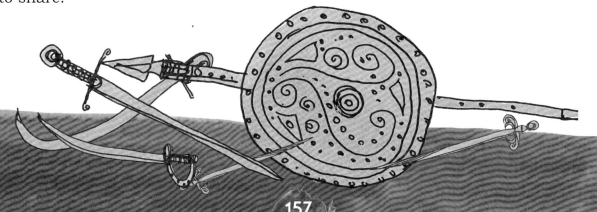